NEYMAR

About the author

Luca Caioli is the bestselling author of *Messi, Ronaldo* and *Torres.* A renowned Italian sports journalist, he lives in Spain.

NEYMAR

THE MAKING OF THE WORLD'S GREATEST NEW NUMBER 10

Luca Caioli

ICON

Published in the UK and USA in 2014 by
Icon Books Ltd, Omnibus Business Centre,
39–41 North Road, London N7 9DP
email: info@iconbooks.net
www.iconbooks.net

Sold in the UK, Europe and Asia
by Faber & Faber Ltd, Bloomsbury House,
74–77 Great Russell Street, London WC1B 3DA or their agents

Distributed in the UK, Europe and Asia
by TBS Ltd, TBS Distribution Centre, Colchester Road
Frating Green, Colchester CO7 7DW

Distributed in Australia and New Zealand
by Allen & Unwin Pty Ltd, PO Box 8500,
83 Alexander Street, Crows Nest, NSW 2065

Distributed in South Africa
by Jonathan Ball, Office B4, The District,
41 Sir Lowry Road, Woodstock 7925

Distributed in India by Penguin Books India,
11 Community Centre, Panchsheel Park, New Delhi 110017

Distributed in Canada by Penguin Books Canada,
90 Eglinton Avenue East, Suite 700, Toronto, Ontario M4P 2YE

Distributed to the trade in the USA by
Consortium Book Sales and Distribution,
The Keg House, 34 Thirteenth Avenue NE,
Suite 101, Minneapolis, Minnesota 55413-1007

ISBN: 978-184831-681-2

Typeset in New Baskerville by Marie Doherty

Printed and bound in the UK by
Clays Ltd, St Ives plc

Contents

Chapter 1
Praça Charles Miller

Handlebar moustache, out-of-control quiff, white shirt, black shorts and football clamped between his hands: the photos from times past, those where a puff of magnesium was used as a flash, provide us with an image of Charles William Miller.

Charlie, son of John, a Scottish engineer who like 3,000 other Brits ended up in South America to help build the railways, and Carlota Fox, a Brazilian with English ancestors, was born in São Paulo, in the Brás district, on 24 November 1874. When he was nine years old, he was sent to Europe to study, as was customary in high society. He arrived in Southampton and started out at Banister Court School before going on to a secondary school in Hampshire.

Banister was a small private school founded by Reverend George Ellaby as a place where captains of the Peninsular Steam Navigation Company could send their sons. The headmaster during Miller's time was Christopher Ellaby, son of Reverend Ellaby. Christopher Ellaby was a passionate follower of football.

In England, the beautiful game already had its official rulebook, with the Football Association having been founded in London on 26 October 1863. This was the first national football federation which brought together the rules of the game. Ellaby, during his Oxford years, was captain of the college team. He passed on his enthusiasm for the game to his students.

Charles Miller was a competent athlete and soon became the captain of the school team. They gave him the nickname 'Nipper' because of his smooth baby face and stick insect body. Despite his build, he became an excellent centre forward and on occasions he played left wing. 'He is our best striker. He is fast, his dribbling is excellent and he has a shot on him like a thunderbolt. He scores goals with great ease,' was how the school paper reported on him. Forty-one goals in 34 matches with Banister Court and three goals in thirteen matches with St Mary's Church of England Young Men's Association, who would become Southampton Football Club, now a Premier League team, attest to this. Miller's style of play was light-footed and a bit on the cheeky side. He had great imagination, superb ball control and a passion for the dummy which left his opponents baffled. So much so that at seventeen he was invited to play for Corinthian Football Club in London, a club set up with players from British schools and universities to match the then superiority of the Scottish teams – Corinthian, a name which, years later, with Miller's advice, would become one of the most famous clubs in São Paulo (albeit it would be called 'Corinthians').

1894. After Charlie finished his studies, he went back to Brazil. In his luggage he put two Shoot footballs, made in Liverpool, a present from a teammate; an air pump to blow them up, a pair of football boots, two football tops (one from Banister and one from St Mary's) and a hefty tome containing the rules and regulations of the Football Association. The story goes that during this trip home Charlie did not stop training, dribbling round passengers and obstacles from one end of the ship to the other. On 18 February Charlie docked in Santos and John, his father, asked him what he had brought back from England. Charlie replied, 'My degree. Your son has graduated with distinction in football.'

The twenty-year-old Anglo-Brazilian began to work, like his father, at the São Paulo Railway Company. He registered with the São Paulo Athletic Club, which had been founded in May 1888 by British communities. There, members played cricket, not football. They knew how to play but no one was interested in it – until Charles Miller started to lay the foundations.

At the club, he explained the rules, and also terminology such as 'half-time', 'corner', 'ground' and 'penalty' to his friends, workmates, and top officials at the Gas Company, the Bank of London and the railways. Eventually he pulled together a group of followers. He convinced them to train on a ground at Várzea do Carmo, between Luz and Bom Retiro, nowadays known as Rua do Gasometro. There were plenty of people who were curious to see what was going on at the ground. Not long after, Celso de Araújo wrote in a letter to his friend, journalist Alcino Guanabara of Rio de Janeiro: 'Near Bom Retiro, there is a group of Englishmen, maniacs as only the English can be, who are kicking around what only can be described as something which looks like a cow's bladder. It would appear that this thing gives them great joy but also great pain when this sort of yellowish bladder enters a rectangle made of wooden poles.'

Sceptics aside, football between gentlemen in the British community was beginning to gain a foothold, and Miller finally managed to organise a match on 14 April 1895. In Várzea do Carmo, two teams made up of Brazilians and Englishmen came together: São Paulo Railway and Companhia de Gás. The 'Railwaymen' won 4–2, captained by Miller, who scored two goals. There were few spectators: friends, managers and employees plus some donkeys that were grazing nearby. It did not matter, however, as it was the first official football match in Brazil. This was the day that the most popular sport in Brazil was born.

It is true that before Charlie returned home to Brazil from England, employees from English companies and British sailors played matches in the street or on the beaches of Rio between 1875 and 1890, with one game being played in front of the residence of Princess Isabel, who ruled the Brazilian Empire under the name of Dom Pedro II. It is true that at São Luis College in Itu, the Jesuit Father José Montero introduced the game of *bate bolão*, a game played by professors and pupils, like Etonians used to. It is also true that games such as *ballon anglais* were played in various confessional and lay colleges in São Paulo, Rio de Janeiro and Rio Grande do Sul. But for Brazilians Charles Miller was *O pai do futebol*, the father of football, because, apart from that first historic match, Miller gave birth to a football club within the heart of São Paulo Athletic Club and his support was fundamental in creating the first Brazilian football federation on 19 December 1901: la Liga Paulista de Futebol, which, one year later, gave rise to the first football league.

This got under way on 3 May 1902 with five teams (São Paulo Athletic Club, Associação Atlética Mackenzie College, Sport Club Internacional, Sport Club Germânia and Clube Atlético Paulistano). SPAC (São Paulo Athletic Club) dominated the first three seasons. With his ten goals in nine matches, Charles Miller was the leading goalscorer for the 1902 season and scored the two winning goals in the final tie with Paulistano. With their light blue and white striped or all white shirts with black shorts and black socks, SPAC retained the title in 1903, again beating Paulistano. The following year, another victory, and Charlie was joint leading goalscorer with nine goals, tying with his teammate Boyes.

Miller played with SPAC until 1910, by which time football in Brazil was played not only by the city-based white elite who saw football as a symbol of modern Europe but also by the lower classes who used football to express themselves – something that was not available to them in other social settings.

An example of the popularity of football was the tour of Corinthian Football Club of London. The English football players arrived on the SS *Amazon* on 21 August 1910. They played three matches, against Fluminense and two other teams, thrashing them all. They then went to São Paulo to play Palmeiras, Paulistano and, on 4 September, SPAC. It was one of the last matches that the then 36-year-old Charles Miller would play.

The English players demolished SPAC 8–2. (They scored several goals in the other matches as well.) 'We did not expect anything else; everyone knows that Corinthian is a team which plays technical football,' wrote the journalist Adriano Neiva da Motta e Silva, aka De Vaney, 'whereas we were, in footballing terms, still sucking on our dummies.'

Footballing issues aside, the most striking aspect was the interest that the arrival of the English team generated. The papers were full of stories about their arrival, crowds waited for the footballers outside the Hotel Majestic and above all were the sell-out crowds at the Velodrome where the matches were played. 'The spectators applauded every move and French perfume filled the air. They were something special, those matches with Corinthian,' reported the papers in São Paulo.

In 1910, Charles Miller hung up his boots for the last time, thereafter dedicating his time to working at the Royal Mail Line. Years later he was to set up his own travel agency, while also acting as the English vice-consul. He married Antonieta Rudge, one of the leading Brazilian pianists, who was to leave him in the 1920s for the poet, Paulo Menotti Del Picchia. He had two children and did not completely lose his ties with football: he refereed, worked as a sports manager and was always a passionate fan of the game.

Charles William Miller died on 30 June 1953 at the age of 79. He saw São Paulo transform itself into a metropolis; he saw *futebol*, which he had introduced to the country half a century earlier, become a national passion. He saw Brazil host the *Coppa Rimet* – the World Cup – and suffered, along with millions of Brazilians, the pain of one of the greatest defeats in footballing history, the *Maracanazo*.

Charles Miller is still remembered today. In Brazilian footballing slang, *chaleira* (the 'teapot', which derives from 'Charles') is the term used to define the move that Miller invented at the start of the 20th century: flicking the ball into the air with the heel, with one leg behind the other. Exactly one year after his death, to represent him in the daily life of São Paulo, the city council gave his name to the square where *Estadio Municipal Paulo Machado de Carvalho* is situated (better known as *Pacaembu* from the name of the area). Today this enormous space in the heart of the São Paulo metropolis, almost like a Greek arena in its shape, is closed off at one end by a zigzag of skyscrapers which loom over the trees and by *Pacaembu* at the other.

Pacembu is a cream-coloured building in liberty style set into the hill. It was opened on 27 April 1940 by the president of Brazil, Getulio Vargas, the city mayor Prestes Maia, and the architect, Ademar de Barros. At the time, it could hold 71,000 spectators. Today, after its refurbishment in 2007, it can hold 40,000. The house of the Corinthians is an absolute jewel of a building: one of the most stunning postcard views of São Paulo. Inside, under the four columns at the main entrance, beneath the gigantic clock, there is the *Museu do Futebol*.

The museum opened its seventeen rooms on 29 September 2008. There are photos, videos, recordings of famous figures in football, memorabilia, souvenirs, odd artefacts and statistics. The exhibition is a journey through the history of Brazilian football in the 20th century.

Hilário Franco Junior, a professor of medieval history, has written a book about football, *A Dança dos dues: Futebol, Sociedade, Cultura* ('The Dance of Gods: Football, Society and Culture'), which has been scrutinised by the football critics. The book summarises the history of football in Brazil from four perspectives: 'In the beginning, football was criticised as it was deemed futile and of no use but it did not take long for the sport to be transformed from a sport for the elite to a working man's game. In the 1930s, there was the first blip. Brazil started to become aware of a social cross-breeding, as it were, as pointed out by intellectuals such as Gilberto Freyre, Paulo Prado and Sérgio Buarque de Holanda. Half-caste, coloured people and white people were starting to live together. There was no need to feel ashamed anymore and if the half-caste could play football, even better. In the 1938 World Cup, the half-Portuguese, half-Brazilian Leônidas da Silva was the leading goalscorer. This was a wake-up call for the country. A coloured player and a half-caste player were there playing in the tournament, despite the requests of those who had asked for them to be excluded.

'The next key moment is *Maracanazo*. This was in 1950, when Brazil were beaten by Uruguay. The playwright Nelson Rodríguez labelled this moment "psychological Hiroshima". Indeed it was. It was a blow to the psyche of Brazilian society and the political classes who had hoped to piggyback on the success of the tournament to gain victory in the upcoming elections. It was a national crisis, but it was turned on its head in 1958: Brazil bounced back and went on to win in Europe. In Paris, the Brazilians chorused, "We are the best in the world!" It was an explosion of national pride.

'From that moment on, Brazil wanted to overcome feelings of national infcriority by being champions again, as they did in 1962 and 1970. But it was not always possible. There was a drought of victories, then the military dictatorship, repression, torture, political opponents disappearing into thin air ... Society looked to football in silence. Doubt was creeping in, despite a couple of triumphs.

'It is a feeling which still pervades Brazilian football today. Brazil appreciates football, it has great players, but it is not the footballing powerhouse it once was. There are other powers in world football and there are excellent players outside of Brazil. Brazil wants to be the Brazil of the future; it feels as though the Brazil of the future has arrived – but then the problems start. Brazil moves forward in a zig-zag rather than in a straight line. It takes one step forward and two steps back. In football it is no different.'

After the professor's lesson, juxtaposing medieval utopias with football in society, we can see this story portrayed at the *Museu do Futebol.* Two schoolkids wait their turn to go in. The noisy schoolkids can get lost in the winding rooms and corridors, briefly stopping where the interactive exhibits allow them to take a penalty and work out the speed of their shot, play on a miniature football pitch, or play table football with little wooden model players who get bashed energetically from side to side.

At the entrance to the museum, a great hall gives the visitor the idea of what football is in Brazil, via a colourful collection of flags, banners, posters, emblems, puppet key rings, gadgets, caricatures, papers, caps and rugs. These are in homage to the passion of the fans.

An escalator takes the visitor to the first floor. Straight in front is Pelé, who welcomes the visitor in three different languages. The visitors are guided from room to room by a series of images of a ball, kicked by a little boy, which skips and bounces from one pitch to another. Baroque angels fly in the dark above. Life-size models of football legends dribble, shoot and shimmy in the air. A plaque reads, 'There are 25 of them, but there could easily be 50 or 100 because they were the founders of football, an art form which is played in Brazil. Gods or heroes, idols of various generations who can be seen as angels whose wings or rather feet take us to places where creativity, poetry and magic is nurtured. They are true angels of Baroque art.' Angels with names like Pelé, Sócrates, Gilmar, Carlos Alberto, Bebeto, Tostão, Garrincha, Ronaldo, Gerson, Rivelino, Didi, Vavá, Romario, Ronaldinho Gaúcho, Roberto Carlos, Rivaldo, Taffarel, Zico, Zagallo, Falcão, Nilton Santos, Djalma Santos, Jairzinho, Julinho Botelho, Zizinho.

A boy called Paulo who came to the museum with his classmates is engrossed by the video of the goal that never was, Pelé against Ladislao Mazurkiewicz, the Uruguay goalkeeper, in the 1970 World Cup semi-final. Again and again he watches it. He then is amazed at the long list of Baroque Angels, name after name. He gazes up at the images and comments to his friend, 'How come Neymar is not here?'

Neymar Jr has not yet risen to this level of football greatness but outside the stadium, under the winter sun, the football shirt which the street traders sell the most of is the gold-and-green shirt with number 10 on it, the one belonging to the latest poet of Brazilian football.

Chapter 2

Prose and Poetry

A conversation with José Miguel Wisnik

Who are the best 'dribblers' in the world and the best goal-scorers? The Brazilians. It goes without saying that their football is football poetry: it revolves around dribbling and goals. *Catenaccio* [an extremely defensive style] and triangulation represents football prose: it is based on synthesis; a collective and organised game, i.e. reasoned execution of the football code.

Writing in a 1971 essay entitled '*Il calcio "è" un linguaggio con i suoi poeti e prosatori*' ('Football "is" a language with its poets and writers of prose'), Pier Paolo Pasolini, film director, writer and great football fan, set out the similarities between literary genres and styles of playing football, offering a significant distinction between football poetry and football prose: a dichotomy which José Miguel Wisnik, Brazilian musician, composer, essayist and professor of Brazilian literature, uses as the basis for his analysis of the game he so dearly loves. He is a huge fan of Santos.

His reasoning is set out in a book, *Veneno remédio: o futebol e o Brasil* ('Poison remedy: football and Brazil'), published a few years ago. Today he reflects on what Neymar means, or what he could mean, for the history of football in his country. This is a player whom he jokingly describes as 'the

Baudelaire of football'. Sitting comfortably in his study in São Paulo, he takes his time before the verbal floodgates open.

'Brazilian football created a tradition which is based on the *ellipse*, a style of play which consists of creating non-linear ways of occupying space and breaching the defence. I based my ideas on what Pasolini wrote about football prose and football poetry. We say that football prose is more linear, more tactically responsible, collective, defensive; it involves counterattack, triangulation, cross-overs and rational movements. The idea of football poetry is that of a football which creates new spaces out of nowhere in a non-linear way, using dribbling as the deciding factor. It can be used to penetrate the opponent's space or just to be effortlessly beautiful or effective. It can be a means to an end or a way to get to goal. Mané Garrincha, for example, took dribbling to the extreme but at the same time was very effective. In the history of Brazilian football, there were glorious moments where dribbling was just for the sake of it but at the same time effective.

'In the 1930s, when Gilberto Freyre analysed Brazil from a sociological, anthropological and historical perspective, he noted that the identity of Brazilian football was closely linked to the identity of the half-caste people. The Brazilians took the English choreographed, formulaic style and turned it into more of a dance, mixing nifty footwork and capoeira and samba dance skills. This obviously has had a huge impact on how our culture is interpreted: the idea that efficiency is only valued if it is accompanied with pleasure; in other words, the ideal situation is bringing together the concepts of work and partying. Brazilian football, in this context, is both the poison and the antidote because it is a form of cultural realisation like popular music or carnival, but it is also a problem because it promotes the idea that our culture glorifies laziness and gratuity over efficiency.'

Can we go back to the concept of football and poetry and how it takes us to Neymar?

'Sure. That was just an introduction. So, Brazilian football gave a style to English football which Freyre defines as curvilinear and Pasolini poetic. A style of play which was developed in South America in the 1960s and reached a climax in the 1970 World Cup in Mexico. At this time, Brazilian football created a repertoire of non-linear moves which can be considered as ellipses, a concept of both geometry and rhetoric. Moves which are based on curves or freezing of time. Just think about all the various types of dribbling: dummies to the left, shimmies to the right, fakes, using the moment to beat your opponent in a static situation. Also the one-two, the lob, the "falling leaf" where the ball would deftly swerve downwards just at the right time. A classic repertoire which existed in Brazilian football from 1962 to 1970. It then existed only as a trait or style but from the 1970s onwards Brazilian football adapted to the new reality in international football, i.e. physical and athletic fitness, team play, different formations and specialisation of attackers and defenders.

'In the World Cups of the 1970s, 1980s and 1990s, Brazil tried various solutions. The football poetry was still there somehow, with players like Zico, Sócrates and Falcão playing in 1982, or with Romario, who in 1994 still played *ellipse* football in a national team which had adopted a more prosaic style. Up until the arrival of Ronaldinho, a footballing genius who brought back the entire repertoire of Brazilian football. You could see Didi's "falling leaf", Pelé's lob or Garrincha's dribbling. Ronaldinho was an artist of mannerisms, almost as though he was "quoting" other players' famous moves. Ronaldinho is well aware of this and as an author quotes another writer, he "quotes" a goal of a player from the past.'

And now we get to Neymar …
'Yes, all of the above was to get to Neymar. In a time when no one believes a poetic tradition exists and that it is disappearing even in Brazil due to a tendency to play football prose, along comes Neymar. A player who represents someone who wants to keep this poetic style alive.

'Neymar has an extraordinary dribbling repertoire. Impressive, I would say: a repertoire that shocks you with its inventiveness, its freshness. It is pure *ellipse* football. If you don't believe me, watch the dribbling with his heel against Seville in one of the first games of the [2013/14] Spanish league season: something unexpected, which no one even dreamed of.

'At Santos, from when Neymar was thirteen years old, he was marked out as the future champion. He is part of a generation which has been trained and grown to be something important. Often important groundbreaking news does not live up to the hype. Neymar, however, completely lived up to the qualities that were ascribed to him. In addition to his magical ability on the ball, he has a natural charisma, extraordinary likeability and the ability to manipulate his public image, just like a pop star. He has conquered the hearts and minds of girls and the public alike and is acknowledged by other clubs' fans and by great players from the past and present. In his years at Santos he showed all his exuberance, all his ability to dribble the ball, thus confirming that the tradition continues with him.

'Yes, Neymar is a poet, a graffiti artist: his sonnets are daubed all over the city's walls. His hair, his way of putting his shirt collar up and his celebrations are all part of his poetic performance. Neymar is a sort of modern-day man of the people, full of energy and life and an absolute star of the current era. He has great vision on the pitch, he has killer passes and he has a superb ability to capitalise on opportunities. He is not just a great dribbler; his relationship with dribbling is not merely rhetorical, as with Robinho who was a poor finisher and whose one-two passes were often just for effect. Neymar has a technologically advanced style, intricate but frighteningly effective. Efficient but without losing its appeal for the spectator. It is on another level, brand new and gives a new dimension to poetic football.

'I see him being in a very interesting situation. Much has been said about him being able to adapt to the *Seleção* [Brazil's national football team]; he proved this during the Confederations Cup. *La Canarinha* [another nickname for the national side] has found a style of play which exploits Neymar's potential to the maximum. The great expectation is how he will fit in at Barcelona. Santos managed to keep him until 2013. Seeing that a player who was at the height of his powers was not sold to a European club or an East European club straightaway was important for Brazil's self-esteem. To be honest, at Santos he was left to his own devices and I hoped he would go to Barcelona to mature in international football.'

Can Neymar's poetry and Barcelona's prose fit together?
'Barcelona's football is not football prose. It is a complete mutation in how to play football in that it combines occupation of space and expansion of the area of play on the wings, which echoes the Dutch style of play, with South American football traits such as the *tiki-taka* heel flick. You could define it as football written in prose, extremely agile but not overly

structured. The presence of Messi and the dribbling which pierces the defence leaves one in no doubt of the determining presence of South American football. I believe that Barcelona, in its great moments, has squared the circle. To bring together prose and poetry, to bring together European football and South American football and to go beyond football's classic dichotomy. What will happen now there is Messi and Neymar? They have different styles. Messi's dribbling is not as exuberant as Neymar's: it is efficient; there is a sense of mystery about the way he moves forward with the ball – you can hardly tell how he does it. He does not move like a Brazilian. His intuition is out of this world, he has a sixth sense for when his opponent is about to present him with an opportunity or when space is opening up. Messi is the straight line to Neymar's ellipse.'

Chapter 3

Mogi das Cruzes

Chaotic traffic: scooter and motorbike horns blasting. Flyovers, skyscrapers, low-level housing, viaducts searing above traffic jams, industry, roadworks, *favelas*. São Paulo, a megalopolis with 11 million inhabitants, seems to go on forever; it seems to want to keep visitors in its clutches and not let them go. The city spreads along the three-lane Rodovia Ayrton Senna, the newest of its kind in the country, dedicated to the eponymous national hero and São Paulo racing driver who died during the Imola Grand Prix on 1 May 1994.

The bus leaves from the Rodoviario de Tiete Terminal (the largest in Latin America and the second largest in the world after New York), with passengers scurrying here and there as they go on their way. The bus is perfectly on time but struggles to get out of the city traffic jams; it scrapes past lorries and cars which dart in and out of the lanes. A toll booth, and it changes motorways. As it heads for Itaquaquecetuba, the city finally lets the bus out of its clutches into the open countryside, which is green and with a plethora of hills that look as though they were sketched out using a ruler. Kites fly high in the sky and bone-dry, dusty football pitches, dotted between the vegetation, mark the *favelas* clinging on to the hillside: red bricks that look like they have been stuck together by a kid playing with Lego, makeshift roofs, satellite dishes, large sheets to cover construction works that have never been completed. Stagnant water, burnt-out cars, kids crossing the motorway on their bikes to get back home with their shopping.

Then the sharp downhill of Serra de Itapey. At the bottom, the skyscrapers of Mogi da Cruzes, one of the Alto Tiete municipalities, an area to the east of greater São Paulo. It was here that Neymar Santos da Silva played football, and here where his son, Neymar Junior, was born: a place with 40,000 inhabitants, its population having doubled in the last fifteen years as commuters have flooded in. They live here and every morning head off to work in the capital; every evening, on the platform at Estação da Luz in São Paulo, they wait patiently to be squashed into the carriages on Line 11 of the Companhia Paulista de Trens Metropolitanos, a creaky and rickety local train which takes them home.

At least there is work in Mogi, where industrial behemoths such as General Motors, Valtra (manufacturers of tractors), Gendau Group (steel works) have plants and employ a large portion of the population. The tertiary sector boasts companies such as Tivit and Contractor, two of the largest telemarketing companies. Agriculture is booming: vegetables, mushrooms, persimmon fruit, medlar and flowers (principally orchids). Stunningly beautiful examples of the latter – in an explosion of colours, whites with shades of fuchsias, violets and lilacs such as the *Olho de Boneca* (*Dendrobium nobile*) – are on show in one of the town's tourist attractions: the *Orquidario Oriental*. 'Oriental'? Yes, you read right: the East.

At the start of the 20th century, Mogi experienced an influx of immigrants from Japan: men and women who worked in agriculture, horticulture and trade. They created a lively and flourishing community that did not lose touch with its roots: there are monuments, restaurants, cultural associations, festivals, schools, and the town has been twinned with

Toyama and Seki. It is a shame that Torii, the Japanese-style gate, symbol of the Japanese immigrants, which was situated at the entrance to the town, was taken down in the spring of 2013 for health and safety reasons. The heavy rains had severely damaged it.

Luckily, one of the other icons of Mogi has not been ruined by the bad weather. A massive shiny sculpture in stainless steel, towering thirteen metres into the sky, at first sight it looks like Don Quixote from La Mancha but it is actually an homage to Gaspar Vaz for the 450th anniversary of the founding of the city. Gaspar Vaz was the rusher who opened the way to Mogi from São Paulo and founded the town in 1560. From Avenida Engenhiro Miguel Gemma, where there is a shiny statue of the adventurer who came to the area looking for gold (or natives who he could turn into slaves), the bus reaches the Geraldo Scavone terminal in a few minutes. Exactly one hour to travel around 50 kilometres between São Paulo and the town.

Through the cobbled streets of Vila Industrial and we arrive at Estádio Municipal Francisco Ribeiro Nogueira, better known as Nogueirão. The large gate is shut but someone comes and opens it. This is the home of União Mogi das Cruzes Futebol Club, a club which celebrated its centenary on 7 September 2013. It was founded by Chiquinho Veríssimo, a white textile tradesman, and Alfredo Cardoso, a black shoesmith. The club was born on Brazil's Independence Day. The football kit is red and white or completely red, with a Tiete valley snake for its mascot (*Mogi* in the local native tongue means 'the river of the cobras').

União is one of the oldest footballing clubs in the region. Over its long history, it has seen the first touches of players like Cacau (now playing for Stuttgart), Maikon Leite (now playing for Náutico) and Felipe (now playing for Flamengo).

It has always been a club which fluctuates between amateur football (in 1947 it was champion of the regional Amador tournament) and the lower Brazilian leagues.

Its golden era was from the 1980s to the start of the 90s, when it fought for promotion to the first division of the Paulista league. However, it did not make it and the only league title it has won is the 2006 Campeonato Paulistão Second Division title. Three years later came its worst year ever: União, or *Brasinha* as it is known in the town, became 'the worst team in the world': eighteen defeats in nineteen matches and 75 goals against, a record which relegated the club to the fourth division. Today it is not doing much better, in terms of either its results or its finances – in fact the situation is so bad that the centenary celebrations were a washout. Senerito Souza, the chairman of the club, said better celebrations may be held in the future.

Meanwhile, the players train for the next league match. At 11.30am the first team play a friendly against the reserves. The sun beats down and the red-brick chimney stack on the far side of the stadium casts its shadow over the green pitch.

On the pitch, behind the metal fencing that separates the pitch from the stands (which can take up to a maximum of 10,000 spectators), sports manager Carlos Juvêncio, or 'Pintado' ('painted' – due to vitiligo which left white blotches on his beautiful black face) watches over the youngest players. When the players get to the changing rooms, I get the chance to have a chat with him.

'How was Neymar da Silva Santos O Pai, Neymar Jr's father, as a player?' I ask.

Pintado replies, 'A good forward, a number 7. He played on the wing; he was quick, skilful, good at dribbling, he always targeted his opponent. He was a cheery chap, extrovert, a nice person, easy to get on with.'

It is a view shared by his ex-teammates, such as defenders Montini and Dunder and goalkeeper Altair. Everyone agrees that Neymar was good with the ball at his feet. An old-fashioned forward who did not score many goals but was good at playmaking and crossing the ball.

Things change when I pose a question about the skills of both the father and son, about what Neymar Jr has inherited from his dad. Pintado, who played alongside 'Pai' in 1993 and 1994, wearing the number 3 shirt for União, well remembers Neymar Jr from when he was just a little boy: 'Pai brought him to training. He was the team mascot.' He recalls how both father and son had the same touch and ability to dribble; Neymar Jr was quicker though, lighter on his feet, faster, more creative. Ex-Seleção goalkeeper Valdir Peres, who played in the Spain World Cup in 1982 and was União coach in 1993 and 1995, is of the same opinion. 'Neymar Jr,' he says, 'is a better dribbler and always looks to finish off his moves and score goals.' 'He has a better technique,' adds Lino Martins, who at the end of his professional career played at União with Neymar Pai and then coached Neymar Jr in Santos's Juniors team.

Neymar da Silva Santos arrived at União Mogi in 1989. He was 24. He was born in Santos on 7 February 1965, the middle son of Berenice, a housewife, and Ilzemar, a mechanic. He has a brother, José Benicio, or 'Nicinho', and a sister, Joana D'Arc, or 'Jane'.

He grew up playing for the Santos Juniors team. When he was sixteen, he moved to Portuguesa Santista where he became a professional footballer. He then began a sort of pilgrimage from one club to another, all of them small fry: Tanabi in the São Paulo region, Iturama and Frutal in the state of Minas Gerais. There, in the south-east of Brazil, Neymar Pai contracted tuberculosis. This put him out of action for a year. He decided to quit football and to go back to work as a mechanic at his father's garage. However, he then received an offer from Jabaquara, a historic club in the metropolitan area of Baixada Santista.

His father was not enthusiastic but Neymar accepted anyway. During the week he worked as a mechanic and at weekends he played. He strung four good games together, one of which was a friendly against União Mogi. The referee for the match, Dulcídio Wanderley Boschilla, pointed him out to the managers of Mogi, who were immediately interested. At the end of the first interview, he was sent to train with the first team. At the end of the second interview with the chairman at that time, José Eduardo Cavalcanti Teixeira, or 'Ado', Neymar signed a contract, for one season, expiring in 1989. 'In those days the salaries were not very high,' Pintado recalls, 'The sponsor was UMC, the University of Mogi. We were paid more or less 350 reais a month but it was enough to live on.'

After years of flitting from one city to another, from one changing room to another, Neymar found himself at Mogi. He was amazing on the pitch and a real success in that A3 league. He played so well that he attracted attention from other clubs in the region. Officials at Rio Branco do Americana, a club in the small city of Americana in the state of São Paulo, were impressed by Neymar when he played against their team at the old stadium in Rua Casarejos and they wanted him, whatever the price.

Despite their loss to União, Rio Branco won the title. A striker was needed to strengthen their line-up. They offered Neymar a decent amount and Neymar was about to accept. It was a one-off chance of a lifetime. União's former treasurer Moacir Teixeira recalls, 'He needed money for his family. He wanted to buy a house for his folks who lived in

Baixada Santista.' Neymar made his wishes completely clear
to the club's managers – who had no intention of letting
him go.

'He was our best striker; he was a great person who
deserved everything he had worked for,' says the former
treasurer. So Moacir, together with nine other União fans,
formed a group to match Rio Branco's offer using their own
funds. The agreement was made on 21 December 1989 with
ten signatories. The group of investors bought Neymar's registration and ensured he could continue to play for Mogi.
The transaction value was 100,000 cruzados novos, 10,000
per signatory, 'and with no interest, with no economic
return,' comments Moacir. In today's money it would be
around 55,000 reais (about €17,000).

This was a lot of money at the time! Neymar was finally
able to buy a house for his mother at São Vicente and
he bought himself a car: a Monza. He felt rich, but
economic and financial reforms introduced as part of the
Collor Plan led to him losing his savings. In the first half of
1990, he played for União; in the second half of the year,
as the club was not taking part in any tournaments, he
played for Coritiba, Cataduvense and Lemense. By this
time, he wanted to have a family. So in 1991, at age 26, in
the church of São Pedro 'O Pescador', in São Vicente, he
married Nadine Gonçalves. They had met when she was sixteen and he was eighteen and a rising star at Portuguesa
Santista.

Their first son was born at 2.15am on 5 February 1992,
in Mogi das Cruzes. Nadine's waters broke the day before
and she was taken to Santa Casa de Misericordia hospital:
an impressive white and pale blue building which stands
out from the city streets. The birth was natural and there
were no complications – mother and son were fine. The

baby weighed 3.78kg, about 8lb 5oz. The new parents found out that it was a boy only when he came into the world – an ultrasound was too expensive for them.

The first doctor to look after mother and son was Luiz Carlos Bacci (now deceased), followed by Benito Klei. It was the latter who discharged them. Being a fan of the club, he knew the baby was the son of a União player, but only when reading the birth certificate years later did he realise that he helped bring the Santos star into the world. 'At that time Neymar Jr did not have the Mohican hairstyle so it was difficult to recognise him,' jokes the director of the department of gynaecology and obstetrics at Santa Casa. The da Silva Santos family was accompanied home by União's physiotherapist, Atilio Suarti. Neymar O Pai had called him and asked him to come and pick them up.

But what was the name of the little baby? Both parents were unsure of what to call him. First Nadine wanted to call him Mateus; his father agreed. They used this name for a week but they were not convinced and, in the end, when Neymar Pai recorded his son's name at the registry, he changed his mind and gave him his own name: Neymar, adding 'Junior'. Within the family walls, he was known as 'Juninho'.

Nadine and Neymar Pai were happy with the arrival of Neymar Junior. Valdir Peres recalls, 'He turned up at the hotel where the club was staying in a euphoric state. He swore that his son would one day be the best Brazilian football player ever.' This was a statement that triggered a whole host of friendly insults and snide remarks.

The da Silva Santos family lived on the fourth floor of block C of the Safira flats, number 593 of Rua Ezelino da Cunha Glória, barrio Rodeio, a middle-class residential development three kilometres from the town centre, built by a metallurgy cooperative syndicate. The pastel-coloured buildings cling to the hillside at the foot of Serra do Itapeti, where the view opens out over Mogi. Theirs was an average-sized apartment paid for by União Mogi. Today not many remember that little boy with curly hair who lived there until he was four. 'They were a quiet, shy family who did not attract much attention,' recalls Licianor Rodrigues, one of the da Silva Santos family's neighbours.

One Sunday in June 1992, after a league match against Matonese, during which he scored the equaliser for União, and before starting training, Neymar Pai decided to go and see his family in São Vicente. He loaded up his car and headed off. Nadine was sitting at his side and Juninho, just four months old, was sleeping on the back seat. It was a rainy day and the tarmac was wet. The Rodovia Indio Tibiriça was a two-way road. It was the long descent down the Serra and it was always tricky and dangerous. Every few hundred metres a sign warned of fog and reduced speed limits: just 40kmph in some places. Suddenly a car on the opposite side of the road tried to overtake and cut into the oncoming traffic. Neymar Pai swerved and tried to accelerate out of the way but he was in fifth gear and the impact was unavoidable. The other car hit Neymar's car head on and wedged itself into the driver's door.

Neymar Pai's left leg ended up on the right: his pelvis and pubis were dislocated. He could not move. Distraught, he spoke to his wife and told her he was dying. The pair looked behind them and Juninho was not there. They thought that he had been thrown out of the car on impact. They thought they had lost him forever. Neymar Pai prayed for God to take his life but save Juninho. Their car was teetering on a ledge, above the river. Nadine could not get out on her side as she would have fallen into the raging torrent below. One or two cars stopped to help and Juninho was found underneath the seat, covered in blood. His parents were beside themselves with fear for their son. An ambulance took them to the nearest hospital.

When Neymar Pai was reunited with his wife and son, Nadine was fine apart from a few scratches. Juninho had a large plaster on his head – the blood had come from a small cut on his head, caused by a piece of flying glass.

Neymar Pai was not so lucky: he had a dislocated pelvis – a serious injury. He had to have an emergency operation. He spent ten days in hospital and then four months at home in bed, suspended from a machine. He was unable to play for almost a year and had to undergo treatment, rehabilitation and physiotherapy with the help of Atilio Suarti and União masseur Antonio Guazzelli. This had been a serious accident, and it affected the rest of Neymar Pai's career. He was not able to regain his touch. However, he did not stop playing. This was his life, his livelihood.

On 31 May 1995 he donned the famous red União Mogi centre forward shirt for a friendly exhibition match. The match was being staged to celebrate the reopening of Nogueirão. The opposition was Santos Futebol Clube, who played in the Divisão Especial (today League A1), whereas Mogi were in Intermediaria (today League A2). At Santos there were players like Toninho Cerezo and Jamelli. Mogi were coached by Valdir Peres and boasted players such as goalkeeper Haroldo Lamounier and Ricardo.

The match put Edson Cholbi Nascimento, or Edinho – Pelé's son – and Neymar da Silva Santos, father of the future Neymar Jr, up against each other. On the one hand, a boy who had listened to the advice of his father on how to behave in life; on the other, a father who was to give to his son (as he continues to do to this day) advice on how to become a great footballer and on how to choose the right career path. Edinho, a goalkeeper, was 25 years old and was playing a routine match. Neymar Pai was 30 and will always remember the match, because it was a match against Santos and he was asked to take the free kicks. Edinho saved his attempts with ease: Neymar bodged them all. A shame. Mogi wanted to win but against professional players it was not possible. The match ended in a draw: 1–1. One goal for Jamelli of Santos and one for Gilson da Silva of Mogi. A good result in any case. The reopening event carried on according to plan.

One year later, on 11 March 1996, the da Silva Santos family welcomed a new member: Rafaela was born.

After many happy years playing for União, Neymar decided to embark on a new adventure. He went back to his parents' house in São Vicente in barrio Nautica 3 for a time, and started to look for a new contract. This time he ended up at Operário of Várzea Grande, Mato Grosso.

The chairman of the club, Maninho de Barros, saw Neymar Pai play for Batel de Paraná. He was looking to strengthen his team. He did not know the name of the footballer who was playing such an excellent match, even scoring a goal. At half time, he asked Laurinho, a striker for Batel, who he was and at the end of the match he met up with Neymar Pai and offered him a transfer to Várzea Grande.

Neymar wanted to think about it, and to discuss it with his family. It was only after speaking to an executive at Operário and learning that he could move his family there that Neymar Pai accepted the offer. He was to wear the tri-colour shirt of Várzea Grande.

His opening match was the semi-final of the state tournament and the hopes of the chairman were realised: Neymar scored and provided the final pass for another goal in the 4–1 win against Cacerense. In the final, Operário faced

União de Rondonópolis. In the first leg, away from home, Neymar did not play and the match ended in a draw. In the return leg on 3 August 1997, Neymar Pai played and the match ended 2–1.

For Operário it was a twelfth Mato Grosso league title. For Neymar da Silva Santos it was the only league title of his career, a career which ended in 1997 at the ripe old age of 32. He felt old: since the accident, his body had not responded as he wanted it to; the pain during matches and training began to hit home. The continuous transfers began to weigh on him and his family. The contracts were less lucrative and he had no hope of achieving anything else in his profession. He headed home to start a new life with plenty of surprises in store.

Chapter 4
São Vicente

Cups, trophies, medals of all types, shapes and sizes from various sports: the display cabinets of the Clube de Regatas Tumiaru are full of souvenirs of past titles spanning its 108-year history.

It started with the aim of 'bringing young people together via sport and in particular water sports'. The club's first premises were on the waterfront in São Vicente, right next to the historic port of Tumiaru from which it gets its name. Today the clubhouse is located at number 167 in what is known locally as 'post office square' but officially is Praça Coronel Lopes. The black and white two-storey building bears the club's coat of arms: two crossed oars, a lifebuoy and the date 1905. We are in the centre of São Vicente, the first city founded by the Portuguese in South America, on 22 January 1532.

São Vicente is a municipality of the small region of Santos and shares the island with the neighbouring city. It is known for its tourism and its trade, attracting hoards of visitors. Of note is the monument celebrating 500 years of Brazil, designed by architect Oscar Niemeyer: a white platform on the top of Ilha Porcha, which provides an incredible view of the coast. It is not to be missed.

The guided tour of Clube Tumiaru is also worthwhile – the city centre site, that is, not the site on the waterfront. There is an open-air swimming pool, training rooms, a gymnasium for *capoeira*, dance, tai chi chuan, judo and gymnastics, and the *futebol de salão* hall. The hall is enormous, with semi-circular vaults, large windows which light the hall, stands to the side, and wooden parquet floor ruined by years of matches. The hall is empty, as it is early morning. Training and lessons take place in the afternoon. Here on this pitch, at age six, Neymar Jr began to play football for a club.

A bola (the ball) has always been his love, his object of desire. His uncontainable passion for the ball is so strong that in May 2012 he stated, '*a bola* is like the most jealous woman in the world. If you do not treat her well, she will not love you and she can even hurt you. I love her to bits.'

He has shown this passion right from when he was a young boy. His mother, Nadine, remembers one time at the market when she was buying potatoes. He was only two years old at the time and 'Juninho' risked his life crossing the road to chase after a little yellow plastic ball. And just like Neymar has said a thousand times, Nadine remembers that he used to sleep with a ball. After only a few years, Neymar had collected no fewer than 54 balls in his room. It was not Neymar's room; more like the balls' room. The room was so full of balls that Neymar had to scrunch himself up in the corner of the bed. *A bola* was even in the photos of his childhood. In one photo of him, taken when he was just a young boy, he is wearing the Santos shirt and under his arm he is carrying a black and white patched ball.

Neymar Pai was amazed that when Juninho was only three years old, instead of grabbing the ball with his hands and shouting, 'It's mine', he gave it back with his feet. For him, football was important, something serious; he had what Brazilians call *jeto*; that is, aptitude, talent. In his grandparents' house in barrio Nautica 3, father, mother and kids all slept in the same room. Between the mattress, the wardrobe and the chest, there was very little space but Juninho made the most of this tiny corridor by playing football. The mattress was perfect for training as a goalkeeper: blocks, dives and saves on the line. When he was tired, he could always use his sister and cousin Jennifer as goalposts while he practised free kicks and penalties.

And yet when Neymar Jr first makes his mark, it is not with the ball at his feet. Roberto Antônio dos Santos, aka Betinho, passionately tells the story of the first time he saw Neymar Junior: 'It was the end of 1998 and I was watching a match on Itararé beach in São Vicente. Tumiaru were playing Recanto de la Villa. I was concerned for my son, I looked around to check where he had gone and a little boy, as thin as a rake, with short hair and stick-like legs, caught my eye. He was running up and down the stands which they had installed for the event. He ran effortlessly, as though he was running on the flat, as though there were no obstacles in his way. He ran without stopping for one second. His fitness, his agility and his coordination made an impression on me. It was something rare for a tiny young boy. This made a difference to me. A light came on in my head. I asked a friend, "Who is that boy?" He told me that it was son of Neymar Pai who was playing in the match for Recanto and had just missed a penalty. I looked at the father: he was well built and had good ball control. I looked at Nadine, who was attending the match: she was tall and thin. I immediately began to think about the genetics of Neymar Jr's parents: they were two fine biological specimens. This made me wonder how the little'un would play football.'

This was the discovery of the star about whom everyone is talking.

56 years old, with a laugh that regularly breaks up his discourse, Betinho is a former right-winger at amateur level.

Born in São Vicente, Betinho works in Santos's youth set-up and travels all over Brazil, indeed all over the world, looking for new talent. In 1990, Betinho discovered Robson de Souza, aka Robinho, in Beira Mar, a futsal club in São Vicente. Robinho now wears number 7 for AC Milan.

In his office on the second floor of Vila Belmiro, Santos FC's stadium, Betinho does not hold back from telling me about the young Neymar Jr: 'At that time, I was coaching Clube de Regatas Tumiaru. I was putting together a team of young kids born in 1991 and 1992 to play in the São Vicente league. At the end of the match, I went to speak to his father to see if he would let me take Neymar Jr to Tumiaru for a trial. Neymar Pai accepted and the boy came with me. The first time I saw him touch a ball, my heart started beating like mad. I saw the footballing genius that he could become. I realised that lightning had struck twice in the same place. First Robinho and now another rare pearl, both in São Vicente. You find footballing talent where kids are most in need. And in São Vicente there are lots of people who come from poor regions. Families who cannot afford to live in Santos because it is too expensive. Here there is a gold mine of talent.'

It is almost impossible to get a word in edgeways with Betinho. But I want to understand how he worked out, from just a glance at Neymar Jr running up and down the stands, that he could be good at football. Betinho's answer is inspirational: 'God gave me the talent to see players who can make the difference and are one step ahead of the rest.'

It is worth noting that by the time he discovered Neymar, Betinho had already been working as a talent scout for five to six years – something which, together with divine intervention and the undoubtedly talented kids of Mogi Da Cruzes, helped him to choose.

But what were Juninho's talents at that young age? 'Football was something which came from the inside for Neymar Jr. At six years old he already had his own style. He was fast and poised, he had great imagination with the ball and could make something out of nothing. He loved dribbling, he knew how to kick the ball and was not afraid of taking players on. He was different to the others, you could have put him with 200 kids his age and he would have stood out just the same.'

Betinho gets up to explain a fundamental concept, starting with music, in particular the samba. 'When I used to put samba music on, I would see him move, gyrate, dance as he did when he had the ball at his feet.' Despite being a little bit overweight, Roberto Antônio dos Santos demonstrates a few steps to explain that without this movement of the hips and legs, you cannot become a great Brazilian footballer. He continues, 'Neymar at that time did the *ginga* movement.'

Ginga is the fundamental movement of *capoeira*, the Brazilian martial art introduced to the country by African slaves, which combines combat, dance, music and corporeal expression. Ginga is a coordinated movement of both the arms and the legs which prevents an attacker from having a fixed target, thus tricking him and making him attack so that the *capoeirista* can then counterattack. The word stands for movement of the body that can represent sensuality, malice, skill or dexterity. The etymology of the word could be the ancient French *jangler*, which derives from the Latin *joculari*, meaning 'joke, pretend and have fun'.

Leaving etymology to one side, ginga is something magical; something Brazilians have in their blood from birth: a gift, an innate talent for movement, for dance, for football, for shimmying, for dummying opponents on the football field. It is the spirit and identity of Brazilian football. And this quality is one that Juninho had in spades at only six years old, according to his talent scout.

Betinho continues: 'What was lacking was strength and stamina, something which is completely normal for a kid at that age. He needed to refine and improve on his skills, his technique, by playing in a team but without losing his passion for dribbling the ball.'

Betinho gave his body and soul to make sure Juninho's skills developed. He took him to play in a futsal tournament in Jabaquara, a nearby town. The team won the trophy. Neymar Jr was the leading goalscorer and the best player of the competition. Betinho also took the young Neymar with him to teams where he coached: Portuguesa, Gremetal and a second spell at Portuguesa.

With curly hair and a few milk teeth missing, and wearing the white shirt with sky blue trim and the coat of arms with the crossed oars on the chest, Neymar started to make a difference on the coloured parquet *salão* pitch. (The game of *futebol de salão*, or *futsal*, where small-sided teams play on indoor courts with a smaller than usual ball, was invented in 1933 in Montevideo by Professor Juan Carlos Ceriani Gravier, who wanted to get his students playing football in a small gymnasium.) He wore number 7, and his Clube de Regatas club membership card, no. 1419, had a serious-looking photo of the young star.

Betinho's hopes were realised. He knew that he had a pearl in his grasp. He continues, 'Neymar was different: he was a very intelligent player. He thought quickly, his mind saw things before the others did. He was always one step ahead. He knew where the ball would end up and how his opponent would react. He took on board my advice and that of the other coaches. He then metabolised the advice and put it into practice. He was the first to arrive at training and the last to leave the pitch. He loved playing with the ball. I cast my mind back to Robinho at the same age and Neymar seemed more talented. I said so to his father: "You have a son who can be one of the greatest footballers. He will be at least as good as Robinho.'"

Neymar Pai, who never got to the top of his profession, believed him and had complete faith in him – though naturally he continued to monitor his son's progress.

Betinho comments, 'Both Neymar's mother and father were close to him: they always followed what he was doing. They treated him with great affection and love. Even if the finances of the family were not the best, they always did what they could for their son. They educated him to be honest, sincere – you know, a good boy.'

But what was he like when he was six years old?

'He was a happy little boy, always cheery, always smiling. He had a nice way about him. He was good at school and he liked studying. He got on well with adults and classmates alike. He was friends with everyone and a born leader. His mates trusted him because of what he did on the pitch. I am very proud of the fact that I was the first coach of a player that is now known all over the world.'

Betinho shows me photos of him with the star, including one Neymar Jr put on Instagram after a match. He also shows me a white Santos shirt with a dedication: 'To my first coach with love from your friend and athlete Neymar Junior.'

That the young man now wears the number 11 shirt for Barcelona is thanks to Betinho and his eagle eyes; his having seen Neymar's potential and opened the doors to the world of football. In turn, Betinho is indebted to Neymar Jr and his family for their loyalty and decency: 'In 2002 when Santos tried to coax Juninho away from the team but without me, Neymar Pai did not accept. He said, "My son needs Betinho at the moment." When Santos tried again and managed to agree a contract, Neymar Pai required that I went to Santos with Neymar Junior. I have Neymar Pai to thank for my job.' Betinho laughs when telling this story.

When asked how he sees his pupil now, Betinho answers, 'As of 2009 when he started playing for Santos's first team, Neymar has been miraculous. He has matured. He has refined his skills. In a few years, he has won individual and team titles. This is the experience he has taken with him to Barcelona.'

But will playing with Messi, Iniesta and Xavi influence his game? 'When Pelé played for the Brazilian team which won the 1970 World Cup, he played with Rivelino, Tostão and Jarzinho. Neymar is a star playing with other stars. I hope that he will soon be the best in the world. Yes, I am sure, Neymar will be better than Messi and after having given so much joy to my country, he will give joy to the entire world.'

Chapter 5
Praia Grande

He cleans his hands with a rag, straightens his hair, then looks straight ahead and, indicating the adjacent construction site, says, 'That there is the best goal Neymar has scored.' Gilberto Leal is a mechanic on the outskirts of Praia Grande. His used tyre shop is right in front of a white wall. On the large tin gate hangs a sign:

Dados informativos da obra. Cesionario: Instituto Projecto Neymar Junior. Local: Jardim Gloria Quadra 27 A y 27 B. Tipo de Obra: Costrução da Centro Social y Esportivo.
(Information about the works. Contractor: Neymar Junior Project Institute. Location: The Garden Gloria Quadra 27 A and 27 B. Type of Work: Sports and Social Centre.)

An employee with a white helmet and blue overalls opens the doors of the workshop to visitors who want to find out a bit more. It is lunchtime: builders and workmen are eating under a makeshift canopy. Two HGVs loaded with concrete pillars and a crane dominate the area which was once a football field, that of Gremio. It is here that the Neymar Institute will be opened in 2014, spread over 8,400 square metres running along the length of the Avenida Ministro Marcos Freire. It is a sports complex with a football pitch, swimming pool, gym, multi-sports hall, auditorium and refectory. The stated aim is to 'contribute to socially disadvantaged families' socio-educational development through sport'. During the first phase it will have capacity for 300 kids aged between seven and fourteen, from poor backgrounds with a per capita income of R$140. In phase two, it is expected that the institute will help 10,000 people of various ages. Gilberto comments, 'It is a good idea. Let's hope that it brings many good things to this area. Jardim Gloria is not a *favela* but almost. Life here is not easy, especially for young kids.'

This verdict is confirmed by two social workers: juvenile delinquency, prostitution, drugs – in particular crack – and lack of prospects are the problems facing the area of Praia Grande, a town with 29,000 inhabitants, twenty minutes' drive from Santos. It is a real problem zone.

On 18 January 2013, the plan for the Institute was presented at the Palacio Das Artes in the town. Neymar Pai and Neymar Jr were on the stage, together with the local councillor who was hosting. 'Juninho' stated that he was very happy with the project: '[We are happy] to be building a space for kids and for the inhabitants of Jardim Gloria. We do not want to discover a new star but rather help families realise a dream and help young kids develop and make plans for their lives. I hope the Institute can serve as an example.'

Neymar Jr is happy to be setting up this place, a place that he would have liked to have experienced when he was kid but no such place existed. He is happy to give back to the people of the area what he and his family got from them. He is happy to do something for the place where he grew up and where he spent most of his childhood. He commented, 'I played on the streets here with my friends: I had great fun in the endless marbles matches; here I played with my kite.'

Neymar Jr moved here from São Vicente with his family when he was seven years old and he lived here until he was fourteen. They lived at number 374 Rua B, Jardim Gloria:

a low-level house, painted in pastel green, at the end of the street, with a corrugated iron roof and a large patio. Neymar Pai built it on a 12m x 30m plot of land. He bought the land using what was left of the savings earned during his footballing career. Two of his friends, Toninho and Jura, helped him. One sourced the materials to build the house and the other helped with labour, all because Neymar Pai agreed to play on Saturdays and Sundays in their teams in Várzea Grande and Baixada Santista.

Today, number 374 Rua B is home to one of Neymar's cousins. As you wander through the run-down area, you realise that Juninho's childhood could not have been easy. 'I am not a daddy's boy. I grew up in a *favela*. My family was humble. We had serious financial problems,' commented the Brazilian icon years later.

After finishing his professional career, in 1998 Neymar Pai took part in an open trial for a job at the CET – the Companhia de Engenharia de Tráfego (traffic engineering company) – in Santos. He was selected and got the job.

Being an assistant builder is not what he wanted, or what he knew how to do: Neymar Pai trained as a mechanic. But for the moment it would have to do. CET was building new canopies for Santos bus shelters. Neymar Pai dug, mixed cement, placed pillars and mended pavements. Four months later he started doing vehicle maintenance and he ended up looking after the Military Police motorbikes. Thanks to Senai training courses, he would become head of department.

He would leave the company in 2009 to manage Juninho's career. But that was in the future: for now, the CET minimum wage was not enough. To make ends meet Neymar Pai sold water purifiers and on weekends he did removals in his trusty old Volkswagen Kombi van (a model famous in the 1960s and 1970s). Nadine looked after the house and the kids but also worked as a cook in a welcome centre for children in need.

Juninho split his time between school and football. He attended the Escola Municipal José Julio Martín Baptista and when the bell rang he would shoot off like a bolt of lightning to football training, where he gave 110 per cent. He played at home, dribbling around chairs and tables and anything that got in his way. He used the door of his bedroom as a goalmouth and tackled the sofa, which knocked him to the ground – penalty. He played against walls, he took the ball on the volley, he headed and chested it and kept it in the air with his thigh, using his left side wherever he could. With a child's size football he scored goal after goal between the legs of the armchair. He imagined various matches: league games, semi-finals and finals.

Sometimes things got damaged. His mother's poor vases took a bashing. Nadine told him off, but not too much. Her father, Arnaldo, whom Juninho never met, had played football. She was understanding and did not prevent her son from having fun with the ball.

The young Neymar did not stop playing football for a moment: he played at home, at school, on the beach with his father when he had a spare moment, and on the street with his friends – a tarmac pitch where the goals were made from any available object and the touchlines were the pavements. The street was on a slope, and every three goals the teams would swap sides to make it fair.

Gustavo Almeida remembers that 'it was difficult to stop Juninho both up and downhill' and he recalls the time when Betinho came to find his pupil to take him to training: 'He parked his car nearby to come and see the match but he forgot to put the handbrake on. The car slowly began rolling downhill and started to gather speed. Luckily we were able to run and catch the car and stop it. It would have been a disaster.'

In Jardim Gloria, many remember Juninho as a shy boy who did not speak much. He loved to collect toy cars; he played on the street, knocking the ball against his neighbours' gates. He trained at the Gremio Praia Grande pitch (where the new Institute is now being built) or in the pitch his father had set up in the backyard to his house. It was grass and it was amazing.

One day Juninho called his friends for a match. There were twenty of them. They started playing at midday and did not stop until six o'clock when it was dark. It was only then that they noticed that the grass pitch had turned into a sandpit. There was not even a single blade of grass. Neymar Pai was bound to be angry: all that hard work ruined in one match. One of Juninho's friends had an idea: he should go to sleep, or pretend to sleep. Neymar Pai would not wake his Juninho. And so, for almost two weeks, Neymar Jr became sleeping beauty: by the time his father came home, Juninho was already in bed.

There are lots of stories of those who knew the most famous neighbour in the neighbourhood. But there are also those who are not old enough to have seen him play in Jardim Gloria but know where he went to school, where he lived or where he played: just like two kids I see cycling home after school, they are proud of someone who has made it, who has become the number one footballer. They also dream about leaving their town one day, just like Juninho …

But let's get back to Neymar Jr's career. Betinho was the one who guided him. After Tumiaru, Betinho went to coach Associação Atlética Portuguesa for a while, as a springboard to get to Escolinha at Gremetal: Gremio Recreativo y Esportivo Sindacato Metalurgicos de Santos.

It is an association, founded in 1972, whose members, in 1995, decided to start a sports project for kids as a reaction to the increasing use of drugs among the younger population in Santos. Today Escolinha de futsal has 200 kids aged between four and fifteen. A large concrete structure with white and blue stripes in Rua Paraná in Santos is the clubhouse. The club crest stands proudly over the entrance.

Inside, kids are training. White shirts against tanned skins on a light blue pitch. In the corridor there is a large green screen which reads 'Silverware of the club. Athletes who have been through Gremetal and now play football in Brazil and abroad'. There are lots of club membership cards with photos and names. From Adriano Bispo Dos Santos (Gremio) to Anderson Carvalho (Santos); from Renatinho (Hangzhou Greentown, China) to Rodolfo (Vasco Da Gama). And, obviously, Neymar. There are four photos of the star, together with his teammates when he played here, and then later with Gremetal's youth squad when he was already famous.

Elton Luiz, manager at Esportes Futsal, explains: 'He came to us in 2001. Betinho took him, together with a group of fifteen kids. He was in a league of his own both on and off the pitch. He just loved playing with the ball. Training was three times a week but he showed no sign of it bothering him. At the club we always try to get all the kids involved and playing. We make them play in all positions, even in goal, and we work hard on the basics. They need to know how to kick with the right and the left foot, have good ball control and work well with their teammates. Let's not forget the relationship with the family. We work closely with parents because our job, at the end of the day, has a social aspect to it. In Neymar's case, his father was very doting. He talked with the coaches to give them some tips, being an ex-footballer himself. We get the kids ready for competitions and internal tournaments and regional championships. When Neymar was here, we won cup after cup.'

He breaks off mid-sentence and asks someone else in the room to go and find the photos of the victories. Here is Neymar, together with his teammates, wearing the yellow shirt with the green collar, crouching, football in hand, and with a smiling Betinho standing behind. Here he is again, with a white shirt and a 'Cascão' haircut, i.e. the one like a sort of toupé which Ronaldo Luís Nazário da Lima sported in the 2002 World Cup in Japan and South Korea. Ronaldo was his idol at that time and Neymar wanted to be at least as good as him. Standing in the photo is coach Alcides Magri Junior.

Alcides is training the under-11s. At the end of the match, he has a few minutes to chat to me about one of his ex-athletes: 'He was nine at the time. He was a smart kid, lively, always happy. I remember his smile and the fact that he was great friends with his teammates. He was a great player and had great skills. When he was on the pitch he changed. Nothing challenged him. He was able to turn a match around on his own. But he did not want to be treated differently to the others. He liked being in the group. When you have a talent like Neymar, often you get jealousy, conflict or envy amongst the players but not with Neymar; there were no problems whatsoever. He was a nice kid, a team player. His teammates admired him. No, Ney was not a show-off on the pitch.'

We talk about his development at Gremetal: 'Betinho worked with him for one or two months and then he came to me at the under-11s team and then the under-13s. This change was due to the fact that Neymar was so good that we moved him up a level almost immediately. He started playing with kids older than him, one or two years older. I remember that when he finished training he went to the technical office and Edy told him, "Hey kid, go and eat in the canteen with the rest of the players", but he did not want to and continued practising on his own. The first title? The Copa Uniligas. The final was against Santos and we won 3–1. Two cutting crosses from Neymar and two goals from Leo Dentinho, then a magnificent ball from Dentinho allowed Neymar to score the final goal. Those two players understood each other perfectly, they complemented each other perfectly. Dentinho with number 10 set up the play and Neymar, number 14, finished off. Or vice versa. They were a fantastic pairing. When they were on the pitch, we never lost. Unfortunately Leo has not had a successful career like Neymar.'

I ask him what a coach can teach to a little footballing genius like Neymar? Magri answers, 'My role was to give him freedom, not block his talent and try to improve his technical abilities. I didn't need to teach him how to dribble …'

And what has futsal given Neymar? 'In futsal space is limited; the player has to think and move quickly. There is no time to stand still with the ball at your feet. You have to dart here and there, pass the ball, shoot. It is a much quicker game than eleven-a-side. The player has to have quick reflexes, be ball smart and have a particular style. Just look at the short and concise dribbling which Neymar employs. In futsal you have to work the ball more, to be more agile and have incredible ball control. This develops into freestyle, which Neymar is such a master of. Let's not forget that 80 to 90 per cent of Brazilian players playing at the highest level, those that get to play for the national team, the *Seleção*, have played futsal. It is an experience which improves the creativity of the player. It means he is more confident when switching to eleven-a-side.'

While we have been chatting, Elton Luiz has pulled out more photos. One by one he points out the players in the teams and the coaches such as Carlos, Eduardo and Amorini André who at Gremetal followed Neymar's development in awe. He points to Neymar celebrating a title. This time his hair is normal but on his forehead he is wearing a white band with writing on it. It is hard to make out but Magri steps in: 'Yes. When he was eleven or twelve years old, he loved playing with a sweatband on his head. His mother had made it for him so that God could protect him, even though his father told him to take it off because his teammates called him 'the masked man'. The writing says 'Jesus is faithful' or '100 per cent Jesus'.

Chapter 6

100 per cent Jesus

A conversation with
Newton Glória Lobato Filho

The church service is over. The priest, Newton Glória Lobato Filho, says farewell to the congregation. He inquires about the health of a relative, shakes hands, hugs a young boy and has a moment's prayer with others. Sunday Mass, in the *Igreja Batista Peniel,* a huge sky blue warehouse in Avenida Martín 781 in São Vicente, was intense and emotional. A real show, lasting about three hours. On the stage, behind the Plexiglas lectern with Jesus written on the column, Newton Glória used every oratory device: from ranting and raving to witty remarks, from a falsetto voice to baritone, from shouting at the top of his voice to a hushed whisper. First he asked the congregation to take part in the 37th anniversary celebrations of the Ministerio Peniel as set out in the pamphlets provided. After the reading of I Samuel 24, 25 from the Bible he started his sermon: a speech with a sentence repeated over and over again: 'God will come and visit you tonight. Prepare your soul for this visit.' The standing congregation answered him with raised palms in an emotional trance. The lights beamed down on the stage below, illuminating a simple white cross, two massive screens to the side, and a large blue, red and yellow banner:

Ministerio Peniel Face a Face com Deus 37 anos restaurando vidas
('Peniel Ministry Face to Face with God, 37 years of restoring lives')

Three TV cameras filmed the sermon, the whole piece to be sold on DVD. There was lots of music, with electric guitars, keyboards and drums. The song was '*Abraça-me*' ('Hold Me'), a religious gospel by André Valadão. The song was sung by the congregation, with the chorus – 'Hold me, heal me, anoint me, touch me' – repeated again and again. With its catchy tune it gets stuck in your head and you cannot forget it.

The members of the congregation approached the stage and the 2,000-strong crowd took the Holy Communion: wine from plastic cups and a bit of toast for the bread. Now the service was almost over but first there was the presentation to the worshippers of a newborn baby and a new couple.

Before letting the congregation go, yellow envelopes were held aloft on the stage and in the wings. These were for the collection of an 'offering to God' with each member of the congregation giving what they can afford. The envelopes are also used to collect the 'tithe'. According to Leviticus 27, 30–32 in the Bible, the tithe is the offering to the temple of the tenth part of the earth's produce and of the flock. Today the tenth part refers to a tenth of a worshipper's earnings.

When the enormous warehouse is almost empty at 9.30pm, Newton opens a stage door and goes to his office. On the wall behind the desk is a framed page of a newspaper: it shows Neymar sporting his Santos shirt. Accompanied by his son, who helps him at the ministry, the minister talks about *Ministerio Peniel* and its famous follower in a calm voice. He explains that in Baixada Santista and the coastal region there are 58 churches and more than 12,000 followers. The majority of them (almost 70 per cent) are young men and women, white and coloured in equal measure. They are schoolgoers, university students or in work. 'But some of them are from difficult backgrounds. They grew up without a family. They have had drug problems and been involved with prostitution. In our church they find support, a new family, an identity, community and the word of God, which can ease their pain. There are lots of them who come here as young kids, as did Juninho. Some get married here, some have their kids baptised here and now they are devoted followers of the church,' comments the Minister.

Let's talk about Neymar Jr.
'He came to our church when he was eight years old. He lived in Praia Grande. The first time he came with his father, and then with his mother, sister and his friends. He was baptised in our church when he was fifteen years old, on the first Sunday of December, 2007, on Gonzaguinha beach in São Vicente. [This ceremony attracts around 10,000 followers every year and they remain immersed in the sea during the christening.]'

Why did he wear that headband when he was a kid?
'It is a sign of faith, a way of paying tribute to his Creator.'

What about the '100 per cent Jesus' band Neymar wore in 2012 during the celebrations for the tricampeonato Paulista.
'I was with him then. It is something we must thank Him for.'

What is Juninho like from a spiritual and human perspective?
'He is a very nice person. Very human. He always says hello and hugs the other followers. He always makes time for the

handicapped kids. He speaks to them, signs autographs and lets them take pictures with him. From a spiritual perspective you should note that, despite his commitments and other problems he may have had, he always came to Thursday Mass when he played for Santos. He sat on the last row and listened to the sermon and the praises made to the Lord. This shows his faith in God and his spirituality.'

Did he ever speak in front of the congregation like some did this evening?
'No. He never did that. One time I said to him, "How come you are on television and you sing, dance or go on stage at a concert but here you are too shy to speak in front of the others on stage?" But he still did not want to do it.'

How did religion help him?
'I believe that all stages in his life are linked to his faith. Throughout all the challenges he faced, I prayed with him and the community prayed for him. Each step he took, each category he moved into, when he signed his first professional contract, when he played his first match with Santos and his first time with the Brazilian squad, we prayed for him. The prayers and the word of God have been a spiritual guide in his life and they have helped him get to where he is today. He could have lost his way as a result of the fame and fortune he has had but it has not happened. The values of the church and his family have been passed down to him and ingrained in him.'

What values did your church give to him?
'Giving glory to God, loving and respecting your family, your friends and your neighbour. These are the values we try to instil in our followers.'

But how do you combine faith in Christ with nights out in nightclubs and relationships outside of marriage?

'It is difficult but this is not only true of Neymar. It is the same with other young followers of our faith who are neither as famous nor as rich as he is. It is an age thing: there are no inhibitions. I pray for people not to have sex before marriage but you need to understand and be tolerant. We need to open our arms and our hearts to the congregation. We cannot shut the door on anyone.'

What did you think when Neymar Jr was nineteen years old and discovered that he was a father?

'I spoke to his father, his mother and to him. I told him that he had to love his child, to help him, because it was his son and a creature of God. In a moment as difficult as this for a young man, his family values passed down to him from his mother and father were of fundamental importance. When David Lucca was born, we presented him to the world here in the church before the congregation, just like we did this evening. His family and his friends were all there.'

Does Neymar pay the 'tithe'?

'He is generous. He began to pay it when he was a young kid. He contributed to the life of the church with 20 or 40 reais. His father and mother paid the tithe for him. He still helps the church every month but he does not pay the tithe.'

Is it true what certain Spanish newspapers wrote a few years ago, that in his contract with Real Madrid or with Barcelona, Neymar Jr wanted to include a clause which covered the costs of plane tickets for you to go back and forth from Brazil, so that he could have his spiritual guide always by his side?
The minister laughs heartily. Wiping away the tears from his eyes, he quips, 'I did not know that.'

How do you see Neymar in this new adventure of life and football?
'It is something natural. It was meant to be. Sooner or later the time had to come when he had to leave Brazil and go to Europe to develop. Neymar can now face this challenge calmly and confidently: he is more mature, he has more experience of the game of life. I remember when he was fifteen, during Mass one time I opened the Bible and I saw the prophetic words of God. God gave me the voice; I asked Juninho to stand up and listen to God's message. I spoke as God's instrument and I told him he would become one of the best players in the world.'

And has the prophecy come true?
'I believe so, yes. I believe the word of God represents the truth.'

Chapter 7

Liceu São Paulo

'When he was a promising talent we believed in him. It was a great privilege to have been able to help and develop one of the greatest footballers in the world. Good luck Neymar Jr.' The poster is fixed with tape to the side of the reception cubby hole at Neymar's old school. Neymar Jr is wearing a red and white top and has a football at his feet. The football pitch is an open book. The advert is simple but effective and works a treat to attract new students to the Liceu São Paulo: a red and white building with five floors, which stands out on the Avenida Ana Costa, a large street leading to Santos's beaches. The school caters for primary, secondary and further education students. It is a private school with a long history. It was opened in the 1920s and is well known throughout the city.

Maria Antonia Julião Faracco, coordinator of the school and head of years six and seven (eleven- and twelve-year-olds) welcomes me to the school. Maria has a little pin on her top with the colours of Santos FC. She is a fan of Alvinegro Praiano and is sincerely saddened by the fact that Neymar Jr has gone to Barcelona, even though she understands his reason for doing so. She shows me down the corridor and calls the lift to take me to the classrooms, the library, the auditorium, the biology lab and, on the final floor, the gym illuminated by light which pours in from large windows – these provide a wonderful view of the city. She comments,

'It is here that Neymar played and it is here that, thanks to Copa TV Tribuna de futsal escolar, he started to become known all over Baixada Santista.' The promotion of the Liceu continues.

But let's talk about Neymar da Silva Santos Junior the student.

'He was an average student; he liked history, and physical education, obviously. He struggled with maths,' says Antonia.

'Numbers and figures were not his thing,' confirms Doña Vilma Julia Rinaldi, his maths teacher, 'but he was not a lazy or disorganised student. He studied hard.'

Maria Antonia continues, 'He was polite, respectful with the teachers and sociable with his classmates. He never missed lessons and never gave us any trouble. The thing we noted was that he was mad about football. You saw it immediately. He was always ready to play a match with his classmates. At break time, students were not allowed to play football but he always found a way around it. He would go to the head-master and beg him to lend him a football so he could take some shots or practise keep-ups. Here in the gym, he and his friends pulled down the volleyball net so they could use the gym as a football pitch. The girls wanted to play volleyball but the boys pretended they were hard of hearing.'

I ask how a boy from a humble, modest family in Jardim Gloria in Praia Grande was able to come to such an expensive private school: surely he could not afford the school fees?

'He won a scholarship,' explains the coordinator of the school.

It is a long story which began on the football pitches of Associação Atlética Portuguesa, known to everyone in Santos as 'Briosa', a company founded in 1917 by a group of Portuguese immigrants. Most of them were builders, working on the building sites all over the city. They did not want to be seen as inferior to Italians, Spanish and Syrians who were setting up their own sports clubs. After having seen an España Futebol Clube football match, they met in a barber's shop to discuss setting up their own club. Portuguesa Santista's sports facilities are only a few hundred metres from Avenida Ana Costa where the school is. Theirs is a massive complex which includes an Olympic swimming pool, a kids' pool, a futsal pitch, party hall and even a *churrasqueria* (steak house). At the centre of the complex is the Ulrico Mursa stadium. Manuel, the association's secretary, reminds us that it is 'the first one in the whole of Latin America to have a roof of reinforced concrete'. The first team, which plays in the second division of the Paulista League is training against a junior team.

In the stands, Edu Marangon is watching with interest the moves of a new kid who has just started and has great potential. Marangon is of Italian origin (his family is from Treviso) and still speaks the language of Dante. He grew up with Portuguesa Santista, played for Torino for two seasons (1987/88 and 1988/89) and then moved to Porto, then Flamengo, then Santos, then Palmeiras, then Yokohama Flugels and finally to Bragantino. He played ten times for the *Seleção*.

Today he is director of sports at Portuguesa Santista. When speaking about Neymar, he says, 'He is different to everyone else. Not only is he a great footballer but he has the intelligence to read the game, coupled with superb physical fitness. For a time, he single-handedly transformed Santos into the *Cirque du Soleil* (the show that children and adults alike want to see at all costs). He is the new Messi.' It is, however, a shame that he has given birth to 'Neymarisation'. Marangon continues: 'Look at all young footballers. They have his haircut, they wear their clothes in the same way, they listen to their music through headsets in the same way, they copy him. If you just stand in front of the door [he points at the entrance to Portuguesa], you will see ten fathers and twenty mothers with a twelve-year-old or thirteen-year-old boy with CV in hand. They all swear that their son is the new Neymar and that they have stopped working to follow their prodigal son's career more closely. But a Neymar is born once every 50 years.' Marangon remembers clearly the boy with the Briosa shirt on this very pitch, playing eleven-a-side.

It was Betinho who brought him to Portuguesa with a group of his boys. It is here that he played his first official tournament on a large pitch. Betinho recalls, 'He played on the left side and immediately showed us what he was made of. He looked for the ball and picked it up in front of the defence. He started dribbling from way back and ran circles around his opponents and then released the ball for one of his teammates or just carried on straight to goal.'

Betinho remembers a goal that Neymar scored in the final of a tournament at Cascavel, Paraná. He reminisces, 'He created from nothing a one-two pass, in the style of Robinho, and then struck the ball which slotted into the top corner of the opponent's goal. A masterpiece. Everyone was amazed!'

The match that many still remember is the junior league match between Portuguesa and São Paulo. Neymar was eleven at the time and his teammates were all twelve. One of his friends, Dudu, with whom he played at Tumiaru and then again at Liceu and had a great relationship with both on and off the pitch, played as the number 11. Dudu started dribbling with the ball and was brought down in the area. Penalty. Number 10, Neymar, took the spot-kick. One-nil to Briosa. It was Dudu again who crossed the ball from the left for Gustavo to score the second goal. São Paulo reacted and Fabio headed in to make it 2–1. But Neymar was on fire. He dribbled the ball and went it alone. Neymar shot but the opponent's goalkeeper parried; Neymar got the ball back and passed it to Leo Baptistão, lying in wait, who slotted in for 3–1. Neymar then finished off the game straight from the centre spot. The goalkeeper read what he was doing but the ball slipped through his hands.

Four-one the final score, with 'Juninho' scoring twice. It was their third victory in the league and took them to the top of the table. At the end of the match, the coach, Betinho, effused praise for Dudu and Neymar in a post-match TV interview: 'He is a revelation for Baixada Santista youth football.' Sporting his '100 per cent Jesus' red headband, Neymar said that the rest of the team played well and, with a cheeky smile, took a swipe at São Paulo: 'We won a lot more easily than we were expecting.' Neymar stood out from the rest to such an extent that São Paulo made an offer. They wanted him in the Tricolour shirt. But no agreement was reached.

Reginaldo Ferreira de Oliveira, aka Fino, coach at Portuguesa and Liceu futsal coordinator, recalls, 'That was a proper team, that one. There was Neymar, Dudu, Gustavo and Leo Baptistão. Juninho loved playing football and always wanted to be the best. The best on the street, the best in the district, the best in the city, then the state, then the country and now the best in the world. He always wants more, every single day, and you could see this in him right from when he was a little boy. Just look at how quickly he adapted from futsal to eleven-a-side. So quickly that within six months Santos had made an offer for him.'

Fino is now a physical education teacher and coach at Escola de futebol Meninos da Vila Ct Neymar in Ourinhos.

'The only one which bears Neymar's name,' he says. 'It was his father who wanted me to train in the school his son founded, perhaps because of what I did for Neymar.'

Among Fino's many accomplishments was that of helping Neymar and his sister, Rafaela, get into the Liceu São Paulo. One day, speaking with Ermenegildo Pinheiro da Costa Miranda, aka Tio Gil, the then head at the Liceu, Fino explained that the futsal team was good but at Portuguesa there were certain players who could make it better. In particular, there was a kid who could make the difference and become the star of the team. The trouble was that his family could not afford to pay the fees. What to do? The head did not hesitate for an instant: 'If he is that good, bring him to the school and we will find a way to help him.'

The trial at the Liceu gym was more than convincing. Fino continues: 'It was Mr Miranda who registered Juninho and his sister at the school. He granted him a scholarship which included all school materials, books, uniform and the school bus for the trip to and from Praia Grande.'

Since 2003, and continuing to the present day, the Liceu has played in the intercollege league organised by TV Tribuna, an affiliated network of Globo TV. More than 80 schools from the region take part and the matches are broadcast on TV. Having a good team and winning the cup is excellent marketing for the school. That is why Tio Gil did not think twice about offering Neymar and his sister a place. In the style of the American universities, the Liceu poached Neymar and the top players from Portuguesa.

Fino continues: 'The first year we got to the final, where we lost against Anglo Americano College. Neymar and Dudu, number 7 and number 11 respectively, were the stars of the team. They were inseparable. Their life was football. So much so that sometimes they would skip lunch to play football. They did not care that they would then have to go to Portuguesa for training.' Neymar was a rising star and the papers began to publish photos and articles about the young kid from Praia Grande. 'Neymar could be next national hero' ran the headline in *A Tribuna*, one of Santos's dailies. The accompanying piece read: 'Neymar is cheeky both on and off the pitch. On the field he strings together pass after pass, he takes responsibility for the ball, he scores and creates goals for his teammates. Off the pitch, he says he is already used to interviews but during the league celebrations he did not manage to dribble past the cameras of his fans and the kisses of his college girlfriends. In the hustle and bustle he almost lost his medal from around his neck.'

The network interviewed him, the kids asked for his autograph and girls shouted out his name. At thirteen he was already famous. This made some schools envious and they accused the school of having taken in Neymar just for football, without enrolling him in lessons. Ermenegildo Miranda went in person to the directorate in Encino to show the register and the enrolment papers to prove the other school heads wrong. Everyone wanted a Neymar in their team.

In 2005 Juninho faced the only upset of his entire school career. He was working with Mateus Pavão Fuschini, the PE teacher at the time. Neymar had little or no spare time and often missed school training sessions. His school teammates were not happy about this, grumbling, complaining and accusing Mateus of favouritism. How could he not train and still be entitled to play? Mateus called Neymar and told him to come to the school training. Neymar came, scored goal after goal and ran rings around his opponents. And that was that. No one had anything to say after that, especially seeing as the school team was on top form with Neymar playing.

The school went on to win the TV Tribuna Cup. A photo

of the time shows Neymar, in his white headband and match-
ing shirt, lifting the trophy (in the shape of a boot kicking
a ball) amid a sea of people. 'We won other tournaments,'
reflects Fino, 'but the televised Tribune Cup was perhaps
the most important.'

Neymar left Portuguesa to join the youth teams at Santos.
In turn, he also left the Liceu to study at the Lupe Picasso
Institute next to Vila Belmiro, Santos's stadium. Maria
Antonia comments, 'And what a coincidence that this year
[2013] the two schools where Neymar studied won the Copa
Tribuna de Futsal. Lupe Picasso won the women's cup and
the Liceu won the men's cup, eight years after that famous
victory.'

Chapter 8

Childhood dreams

A conversation with Leonardo Carrilho Baptistão

'Who could have imagined that our childhood dreams would have come true! I wish you all the best in life ... I am with you Léo Baptistão.'

Neymar published this message with two photos on his Instagram profile on 21 August 2013. One photo shows him with a red headband on and wearing the Portuguesa Santista shirt, standing bolt upright next to a teammate who is taller than him and is squinting in the sunlight. The teammate is Leonardo Carrilho Baptistão. In the other photograph he is holding the Barcelona pennant and shaking hands with the number 27 for Atlético Madrid – Leonardo Carrilho Baptistão, better known as Leo Baptistão.

Here are two Santos kids whose paths have crossed again in Madrid during the first leg of the Spanish Super Cup. Both of them have achieved their dreams.

Leo comments, 'Neymar made it before I did. When I arrived here, he was already training with the first team for Santos. Meeting up again as professional players in one of the best leagues in the world has been very emotional. We talked about the match during the warm-up and again at the end of the match. He was happy for me and for where I had got to. He told me to say hello to my family and my father, Aroldo, who is good friends with his father.'

It is at the cafeteria of the Ciudad Deportiva de Majada-honda, Atlético's training ground, where Leo Baptistão, aged 21, unshaven and with ruffled hair, meets me after training to tell me his past and that of Neymar: parallel lives and with many things in common. They were rivals, teammates and then, after a short period apart, rivals again but on another continent.

Leo explains: 'I was number 9 in the futsal team in my school, the Colegio Jean Piaget; Neymar played for Liceu São Paulo. We met in the semi-final of the Tribuna TV Cup in 2004. I scored the first goal. Neymar equalised. I made it 2–1, and Neymar equalised. It went to penalties. I missed mine and we were eliminated. They went on to the final, which they lost against Anglo Americano College. It really gave us purpose playing in the TV Tribuna Cup because the opening match, the semi-final and the final were televised. What do you expect? Everyone wanted to become professional football players, we were glued to the TV when there was a match on; we saw the professional players being interviewed and now it was happening to us, kids of eleven or twelve. At the end of the match, the TV crew came over and stuck the camera in your face and interviewed you. We were beside ourselves with excitement.'

The Tribune Cup was not the only time you found yourself up against Neymar ...
'No. It happened in the Santista league [the regional league]. Neymar was playing for Gremetal, I was playing for Santos where I had been since eight years of age. Prior to that I was at Saldanha. The semi-finals and finals were always a private affair between our two teams. In this league Neymar and I finished the season as equal lead goalscorers, both scoring 24 goals. I remember it well because it was my

first individual trophy in futsal. Then we were called to the Santista trials and we got to know each other.'

And you played together at Portuguesa Santista.
'Yes. We arrived at Briosa more or less at the same time. He came from Gremetal under Betinho's guidance; I came from Santos. We played together in the futsal team and in the eleven-a-side team. We were second in our league. It was a good time. There were lots of kids like us born in 1990, 1991 and 1992 who showed promise. The youth teams at Santos were at full capacity, the coaches were talented and the stands were always packed. I remember a match with São Paulo in which Neymar scored two penalties and made the final pass to me for another goal. The Ulrico Mursa stadium was crammed full. Unfortunately it is no longer like that. Briosa is in decline. Portuario, where Robinho played, is not doing well and even a great football school like Jabaquara is suffering.'

Let's go back a bit, to the team you played in when you were twelve years old.
'It was incredible. We passed the ball around without even looking where the other player was. We knew exactly how we all moved. There was a perfect feeling between us. It was very easy to play because we were friends, we had been together for ages and we grew up playing futsal. The smaller pitch helps you to think quickly and to have great ball control. Our coach, Fino, knew a lot about football … he knew how to intervene during a match when things were not going according to plan, when the other side were dominating; he taught you how to defend, to mark the other player and to attack. He used to pull me to one side to make me kick with the instep of my foot, on the volley; he insisted on the

basics and technique. He helped me become what I am and he also helped Neymar a lot.'

But what was Neymar like at twelve?
'He was the best player on the team. He did incredible things with the ball: dribbling, one-two passes, left- and right-footed lobs. He was cunning; he did things way above his age. Everyone knew that he would become a star. If the expectations for me or for others like Dudu or Gustavo were normal, or rather becoming a professional footballer for us was a distant dream, for Neymar his future as a star was clear.'

How come? What was different about him?
'What he does now on the pitch, he was already doing at the age of ten, eleven. Let's just say that the tactics for lots of matches were to just pass the ball to Neymar and let him get on with it.'

Really?
'Yes, really; and before, when I played against him, the coach and the players put together a strategy whereby Neymar did not get the ball, so as to block him and shut him out of the game, so that Neymar could not play his game.'

Let's carry on with your parallel lives.
'Fino brought Neymar, Dudu and other kids with him from Portuguesa to Liceu São Paulo. He wanted me to come but I preferred my school, which was close to home.

  'Neymar left for Santos and I continued with Briosa. From that point, our paths went their separate ways. At sixteen, thanks to a friend of my father, I came to Madrid for a trial with Getafe and then moved to Rayo Vallecano. I fell ill – a severe case of hepatitis. I went back to Brazil for treatment and then back to Spain, to Madrid, at Vallecas. From that point on, we are down to the last two years. In the 2012/13 season I played in *La Liga* for Rayo. I played well and in June 2013 I came here to Atlético.'

Is it difficult to settle in Spain?
'It was hard. Especially at the beginning. I was a young kid and I found myself in another country with a different culture, a different language, far away from my friends and family.'

And how about adapting to Spanish football?
'Coming here so young helped me a lot. I played with other kids who were learning just like me.'

And in your view how did Neymar fit in to La Liga and Europe?
'A footballer like him does not need to adapt; he already fits in. He is showing it already, just look how relaxed and happy he is and he has great players all around him. They said he would not get on with Messi, Iniesta, Xavi but they were wrong. Because Neymar is a nice guy, humble – he is not a show-off. Even when he played for Portuguesa, he never said he was worth more than the other players; he just wanted to play and train. And if someone criticised him for his behaviour, he apologised to everyone.'

On the subject of criticism, they accuse him of going down too easily. You know, he dives and overeggs it.
'There are times when he dives, like all players, but if he didn't he would hurt himself. He is not someone who goes down at the slightest touch, nor a drama queen. And I don't agree with those who say that his style, his dribbling, provokes his opponents. What he does is part of football. It is

not a provocation; it is tricking the defender: impress him so that he thinks, "He threaded it through my legs, he lobbed it over me – how can I stop him?" Neymar's football is a spectacle. There are few players in the world that can give you a show. He does and he does it well and he does it every single match.'

The conversation is interrupted. Luis Edmundo Pereira, a former defender who played for Palmeiras, Atlético Madrid and *La Canarinha* during the 1974 World Cup, stops to say hello. He hears we are talking about Neymar and gives us his view: 'He is phenomenal! People need to stop talking about his "theatrics" once and for all. They lay into him, they go in hard wherever he plays; he gets fouled more than many other players (as shown by the statistics) and yet, these know-it-alls think he should stay on his feet. Let's look at how many times Di Maria or Arbeloa go down! No, it is just gossip-mongering. Let's tell things how they are: here, as always happens in this country, it starts with the eternal rivalry between Barcelona and Madrid. That's why even José Mourinho gets involved in the debate, accusing Neymar of being a *piscinero* ('pool attendant') and asking UEFA to get involved and sanction him.'

Having aired his thoughts, Pereira heartily pats Leo on the shoulder and heads off.

Juanjo Anaut, the Atlético press officer, gives a sign that our time is nearly up. One minute left.

How do you see your and Neymar's future?
'Neymar's future is the Brazilian national team and Barcelona. In the Confederations Cup, everyone thought that Brazil would not have beaten Spain but Brazil thrashed them. Neymar was the star. Now with Neymar playing, Brazil

is one of the favourites for the World Cup. He will stay at Barcelona for a long time because he enjoys it and the people love him. As well as being a great footballer, he is a nice guy.'

The future of Leo Baptistão, on the other hand, has changed tack. He has moved from Atlético Madrid to Real Betis Balompié. On 11 January 2014, he was announced as the Seville club's new signing.

Chapter 9

Santos

The harbour, coffee houses, beaches and football. This and much more is Santos: a coastal city with around 500,000 inhabitants in the state of São Paulo, 68 kilometres from the capital. Endless convoys of HGVs loaded with containers and goods wind down the Serra do mar along the Rodovia dos Imigrantes to queue one behind the other at the entrance to the thirteen square kilometres of port, the largest in Latin America. A quarter of everything that comes in and out of Brazil passes through this port – goods and passengers. The transatlantic cruise ships of the largest companies offload hundreds of tourists here for a few hours. A quick visit to the city and then off again. Ships, petrol tankers and cargo ships which embark and disembark to and from the open sea or moor along the coast, their lights flickering on the horizon of the night sky in Baixada Santista.

Copper domes, coloured glass depicting the mythology of the country, marble mosaics, granite columns, groups of sculptures, a clock tower 40 metres high: the Bolsa Oficial de Café in Rua XV de Novembro no. 95 is a monument to the coffee heritage of the city, a testament to the golden era when Santos was the main market for the world coffee trade – so much so that certain countries only bought coffee if it had been certified here. The Bolsa opened on 7 September 1922 and for almost 50 years the shouts and cries of the traders bargaining for the seeds from the *Coffea* trees could be heard. Nowadays it is a museum – a city tourist attraction – a bookshop, and a crowded coffee house where different aromas can be experienced.

It is a meeting point in the historic centre which, with its paved streets, lampposts and pastel-coloured buildings built at the end of the nineteenth and beginning of the twentieth century, shows the trappings of the coffee economy. Here, on 16 February 1867, the first train of the São Paulo Railway arrived, connecting the production areas with the port: the point of departure for Europe and point of entry for immigrants, Italians and Japanese, who came to replace the African slaves in the plantations. Today the port is still a source of wealth, alongside fishing, trade and tourism. Santos has a flourishing economy, which in the next few years could be propelled by natural gas and crude oil. In 2008, the Carioca reserve was discovered in the Santos Basin. It is believed to contain 33 billion barrels of crude oil. It is the third largest reserve in the world. It would enable Brazil to not only be an agricultural economy, exporting coffee, sugar, soya and ethanol, but to become a petrol powerhouse.

That is for the future. For now, let us look at the present-day Santos. It is a city which comes in at fifth place in the quality of life rankings for Brazilian municipalities according to the UN Development Index, which considers education, GDP per capita and life expectancy. A city which, like the rest of the country, shows the brutal contrast between the rich and the poor, between the gleaming coastal buildings and Vila Gilda, the largest *favela* of stilt-houses in all of Brazil; between the slightly run-down historic centre where the street lights are switched off at night and the beaches on the other side of the tunnel, which are brimming with life and activity.

The beaches: seven kilometres of fine white sandy

beaches crowned by skyscrapers. Glass and concrete, dream penthouses, rooftop pools. Pinnacles, one next to the other, each more stunning than the next. A neat line which every so often is broken by neoclassical hotels from the 1920s – the first hotels to host travellers who wanted to benefit from bathing in the sea.

Shopping centres, restaurants, bars, cycle paths, tourists, OAPs jogging, young men and women going back and forth laden with surfboards, boules players and beach volleyball players. It is a constant to and fro of people in Praia Gonzaga.

On Saturday evenings, the beach becomes one big football pitch. One match after another as far as the eye can see. Lines drawn in the sand and matches played barefoot. All ages play: pot-bellied elderlies sweat and groan; fit, handsome young men; teenagers darting around and young kids pulling one trick after another. There are shouts, fouls, goals, penalties and throw-ins with balls that skim dangerously close to the massive waves of the Atlantic. There are coloured shirts of all the great Brazilian and European clubs, bare chests and makeshift kit. Five-a-side, eleven-a-side, foot volley, 'futebol society' (seven-a-side): not a single football-related game is missing in this procession of sport.

Soon it is evening and the beach slowly returns to its natural state. With goalposts and crossbars slung over shoulders, nets stuffed into bags, the footballers leave and are replaced by the laughter which burbles out of the beach bars, and by the tramps who methodically pick up bottles and cans.

Football returns to the clubs, the suburban pitches, the futsal halls, the youth clubs. It returns to the fans and to the three city football clubs: Portuguesa Santista, Jabaquara, and Santos, the club that changed forever the way football is played, according to its famous supporters' group, the Torcida Jovem.

'One hundred years of football art' is the slogan the club created for its centenary in 2012. These words can be found at the entrance to the Urbano Caldeira stadium, better known as Vila Belmiro, after the area. It is a small sports complex, opened in 1916, with capacity for 16,798 spectators. During bad times, no more than 4,000 turn up.

Everything is close to hand. You can almost touch the pitch and the players. At the heart of the stadium lie the changing rooms. A plaque marks the entrance: *Vestiario Edson Arantes do Nacimiento Pelé* ('Edson Arantes do Nacimiento Pelé Changing Rooms'). Inside is a large photograph of the great number 10: an homage to 'O Rei'.

Pelé is not the only champion whose successes are on display. In the changing rooms, each locker bears the photo of a current player and the name of one of the *Alvinegro* icons.

The history is set out over the 380 square metres of the Memorial das Conquistas on the ground floor of Vila Belmiro. Photos, footballs, autographs, football boots, newspapers, plaques, shirts and trophies representing 100 years of football.

It was on 14 April 1912 when the largest, most luxurious transatlantic liner in the world, RMS *Titanic*, collided with an iceberg and sank in a few hours. Of the 2,223 passengers, 1,518 lost their lives. In Santos, that same Sunday, 39 young men, aged between fifteen and 24, some students, others workers, all members of the well-off upper middle classes, met in the grand hall of the Club Concordia. Santista sportsmen Francisco Raymundo Marques, Mário Ferraz de Campos and Argemiro de Souza Júnio had called a meeting to found an 'important football club'. The meeting went on for a long time. It was difficult to agree on a name that hit the mark, that pleased everyone. Someone suggested Africa Futebol Clube, others Concordia, others insisted on

Associação Esportiva Brasil; and then finally, at 10.23pm, the simplest idea of all was agreed as the name of the club: Santos Football Club (in the English style, naturally).

The next day the *Diario de Santos*, edited by Tito Brasil, splashed the news all over the front page with the headline 'Sports', wishing 'a long and prosperous life to the new sports club'.

On 15 September 1912 the new team played at the pitch in Avenida Ana Costa, no. 22, where today the Igreja Coração de Maria stands. This was the first official match. The opposition were Santos Athletic Club. The final score was 3–2 to the new team. The next year Santos were invited to play in the Liga Paulista de Futebol, the first official competition. The first match was against Germânia, on 1 June 1913. One goal for and eight against – a thrashing by all accounts. If this was a sign of things to come, it was not looking good.

In fact, 22 years passed before Santos achieved their first title, winning the Paulista league in 1935. Professional football in Brazil had been around for two years by that time. It was that same year, during a match at Vila Belmiro against São Paulo da Floresta (the team which became the current São Paulo) on 12 March, that the Santos fans claimed for themselves the nickname which they had been given by other fans. Every time Santos played at São Paulo, the home fans teased the Santos fans by shouting 'rotten fish, fishmongers'. When they played São Paulo da Floresta that day, they had had enough, and retorted, 'We *are* fishmongers and we are proud of it'.

Peixe ('fish') became the nickname for Santos and a killer whale became the club mascot. But the killer whale had no bite, as, after the first trophy, a long barren period ensued. It was a dark time for the club, which writer and commentator José Roberto Torero defined as 'our middle ages'. He was not wrong: another twenty years passed before Santos won the league again. By then it was 1955 and a team made up of Manga, Hélvio, Feijó, Ramiro, Formiga, Urubatão, Tite, Negri, Álvaro, Del Vecchio and Pepe beat Taubaté 2–1 in the final.

Then in June 1956, a fifteen-year-old boy arrived at Vila Belmiro, accompanied by former *Seleção* footballer Valdemar de Brito. Born in Três Corações in the state of Minas Gerais, the boy was called Edson Arantes do Nacimiento. Yes, Pelé; who, together with Gilmar, Dalmo, Mauro, Calvet, Zito, Mengalvio, Lima, Dorval, Coutinho, Pagão and Pepe, made Santos into a team famous all over the world and Brazilian football the benchmark for footballing excellence.

The end of the 1950s and the 1960s were the golden years for the club: nine league titles, five Brazil Cups, two Coppe Libertadores and two Intercontinental Cups. Santos was also the basis for the Brazil team which won the 1958, 1962 and 1970 World Cups.

The explosion of football in this period was in line with what was going on in the world. It was in harmony with rock 'n' roll, The Beatles, the bossa nova (a style of samba mixed with jazz and classical music which influenced the world). Brasilia was founded in this period: a city with futuristic architecture, a symbol of the Brazil to come, capable of originality due to its *mestizo* ('mixed blood') origins – hopes which were abruptly dashed not long after with the military coup d'état of 31 March 1964 and the years of dictatorship which followed.

Futebol, the art of football, the Santos style, developed in the years of change and hope, continues to amaze nonetheless. Pelé is the undebated icon, the pride of the nation, the player who scored 129 goals in 1959. The game played by *Alvinegro Praiano* was football art, a show in its purest form, an expression of the joy and pleasure of football. It was something everyone wanted to see up close. And so Santos became a sort of Harlem Globetrotters, touring in 59 countries and even stopping a war in January 1969 when, during a tour in Africa, they managed to get the factions to lay down arms in the Congo; similarly, their visit to Nigeria later that same year resulted in a temporary truce in the Biafran war.

On 19 November 1969, in a Silver Cup match (the precursor to Brazil's national league competition, the *Brasilerão*) against Vasco da Gama in front of 65,157 spectators at the Maracanã in Rio, the 'Black Pearl' scored a penalty. It was his 1,000th goal. 'The entire world applauds the greatest footballer of all time,' the radio commentator said.

Five years later, the saddest day occurred. On 2 October 1974, Santos played against Ponte Preta at Vila Belmiro. In the 22nd minute, Pelé took the ball in his hands, kneeled down at the centre of the pitch and raised his hands to the sky and faced each side of the stadium. Teammates and opponents waved at him. He got up, took off his black-and-white-striped shirt, ran a lap of honour around the pitch and left in tears for the changing rooms while the whole stadium sobbed. After nineteen years, O Rei had left Santos.

'Brazil is Pelé's widow,' reflected the TV reporters. It was a hard event for the country, and Peixe, to swallow. So many years of marvellous football ended in that moment. A period of grief ensued. The story of Santos continued, but their rebirth would take four years. Only in 1978 did they once again find success again in the Paulistão, with the team of Juary, Pita, Ailton, Lira, Nilton Batata and João Paulo: the young and exuberant *Meninos da Vila* ('young kids of Vila Belmiro').

*   *   *

Emerson Leão, the coach who arrived at Santos in 2002, gave the kids of the club's youth teams a chance, just like Lula (Luis Antonio Perez) had done in the 1950s and 1960s. History repeated itself. Santos was reborn with the second generation of *Meninos*: Diego and Robinho, who took Santos to their seventh Brazilian championship in 2002 with lively and showy football. And eight years later came the third generation of *Meninos*, led by Neymar.

In honour of Pelé, the Memorial das Conquistas at Vila Belmiro dedicates an entire cabinet to memories and emotions. The only other player who is honoured in this way is Neymar. The two champions, side by side. A shiny tin statue with Mohican hair for Neymar, a copper-wire statue with the Brazil number 10 shirt for Pelé.

Chapter 10

Peixe

José Ely de Miranda, aka Zito, and Antônio Lima dos Santos, aka Lima, are two icons of Santos Futebol Club. Zito, nicknamed 'O Gerente', arrived at the club in 1952. He had a small moustache like Clark Gable, and wore number 5 on his shirt. He was captain of a dream team which won everything there was to win in the 1950s and 1960s. And we must not forget that he won the World Cup with the Brazilian national team in 1958 and 1962. They say he was the only player able to give orders and shout at 'O Rei', the king, Pelé.

Lima played with Santos for ten years from 1961 to 1971, appearing in 696 matches, scoring 65 goals and winning every title. They called him 'O Curinga' ('the joker in the pack') because he played in every position on the pitch except in goal. He was the 'lung' of that famous team which amazed the world.

Zito and Lima were two key figures in Neymar's life. The first introduced Neymar to Santos; the second was his coach on the eleven-a-side pitch.

Zito is 81 today. His hair is white and his moustache has gone. His health is a bit hit and miss at times but his memory is perfect. He remembers well the first time he saw 'Juninho' and decided that the boy had to play for Santos. It was the end of 2003. At that time Zito was the coordinator for the junior teams for Santos. A Santos fan, Alemão, who was obsessed with Peixe, called him to tell him that he should go and see a certain Neymar, a young boy who was playing in a futsal tournament. Alemão added, 'He is only a kid but he plays very well. I am sure you will like him.'

Alemão is a notable character. He has thirteen Santos crests tattooed on his arms and one on his forehead. He manages a bar in front of Vila Belmiro and is a leading figure in the official supporters' club. When he saw Neymar, he saw his potential. But he wasn't the only one: lots of people had tipped off Santos about Neymar, the boy from Mogi da Cruzes. Another of these was José Luiz Pinho, a metallurgy trade unionist, who had watched the boy closely when he played on the parquet at Gremetal.

Regardless of who spotted him, Zito decided to go and see this player. He spoke to a friend and went to the Portuguesa Santista ground.

Zito says, 'I have to admit that Neymar filled me with joy. He was only eleven years old but he did the same things then as he does today. With the ball at his feet, he was incredible, sensational. He was miles above the rest. A real superstar. I went back to Vila Belmiro and I spoke to the chairman, Marcelo Teixeira. I told him that we had to get Neymar straight away before someone else snatched him up. I insisted that Neymar signed a contract which tied him to Santos for a long time. When you see a player you like that much, you know you can't be wrong. I was sure he would bring great happiness to Santos's fans.'

And so a few months later, on 10 May 2004, Neymar da Silva Santos Jr signed his first contract with Santos, for a five-year term and a salary of 450 reais per month. It was his first salary, even if he had already earned bits and bobs here and there and received a few presents for his family when he was playing for the futsal teams.

When Neymar started his Santos career, the club had no

eleven-a-side team at under-13 level; so he started in five-a-side. (The efforts of Zito and the chairman led to the creation of such teams thereafter, in order to train talents like Neymar. In 2006, the Centro de Treinamento Meninos da Vila was opened, set up specifically for the junior teams of the club.) It was Lima who brought him to eleven-a-side. He recounts: 'I had heard that he was a good player but, unfortunately for me, he was playing futsal. I went to see him train and decided to get him to join my team made up of fifteen-year-olds, whereas he was only twelve. I spoke to Zito: "Look, if it's ok with you, I'll take Neymar in my team." His reply was clear: "Are you mad! He is not strong enough yet to play eleven-a-side." I insisted, however, and explained that I did not want him to play in the league: I just wanted him to train with the group at a different level. Zito agreed: "OK, you're the boss, do what you feel is right." And that was that. Neymar came to play for me.'

Behind his desk in his office in Vila Belmiro, the deep-voiced, stocky Lima remembers the details of those first years on the pitch: 'He played centre forward. I reflected on this and I told him that with his physique he was not able to move well in the area against defenders who were bigger and stronger than him. It was the only thing I had to tell him in three years. I suggested that we mix things up a bit and that he move to midfield, so that he could receive the ball, be in front of the defence and attack and use his speed. That way no one could stop him. I told him, "You can zig-zag your way through the field and finish off the move or assist your teammate who is in a good position." Neymar was having none of it. At the beginning, with tears in his eyes, he said to me, "No. Profe. You want to take me out of the area; you don't want me to score." But I explained to him that it was quite the contrary and that I wanted to place him in area where he could dominate the ball. That way he would not have to take the ball from behind him, turn round or deal with taller and bulkier players.'

Players like the famous *gatos del futebol* ('football cats'): kids who were way too old for the category. Bruisers who went in hard to intimidate smaller and more fragile opponents like Neymar.

It was Neymar's build that worried Zito. 'He was not wrong,' reflects Lima. 'Look at how he is now. You can imagine what he was like six or seven years ago. He was pretty thin, but, thanks to the work of the club, bit by bit he gained seven to eight kilos of muscle mass and a top-rate physique.

'At barely fourteen, Neymar was playing in the fifteen-year-olds' league. He played futsal and eleven-a-side. In the morning he trained on the pitch and in the evening on the track – maybe a bit too much, and I told Zito and Neymar Pai as much. I wanted him to choose and in the end he did.

'Neymar was a quiet, polite and obedient child. It was easy to work with him. He never complained about any of the exercises: basics, finishing, physical. Training was not a burden for him. I remember that when it was time to leave the pitch and go to the changing rooms for a shower, you always had to wait for him. 'Profe. Just five more shots. Let me take this free kick,' he used to say.

'He was so determined, which is so important at that age. When I explained to him what I wanted from him from a training session, you could be sure that Neymar would always achieve what you were trying to achieve. Just like the time when for the entire week we tried and retried a set piece to exploit his speed. We got to the match against San Bernardo. I settled myself on the bench and spoke to the reserves. I had my back to the pitch. I heard shouting and I was not sure what was going on. Then one of the reserves said, "Profe.

Neymar has just scored using exactly the set piece we practised all week." It was incredible.

'The only thing he did not like doing was kicking or
shooting with his left foot, because he was right-footed.
When I insisted, he complained. He did not want to hear
about shooting with his left. "Why always me, why do I always
have to do it, Profe?" he said. Today he is ambidextrous. I
text him every now and then to take the mickey, just like I
did after the goal in the final of the Confederation Cup. The
message read something like "Not bad for someone who did
not want to shoot with their left".'

Lima goes quiet for a minute and then says, 'I am certain
that he will not take long to become the number one in
the world' – words of honour indeed coming from a champion who has seen hundreds of players and who has himself
played with the best of them all, Pelé.

Now we have heard the views of the coach, what about
those of Neymar himself? What did Juninho dream about
becoming when he started at Santos?

In 2004, Antonio Venancio, a Brazilian researcher,
received a request from someone in England to interview
some of the most promising players at Peixe, those who
could become the next Robinho. The interview was to serve
as the basis for a documentary on Robinho, who at that time
was expected to be the next Pelé – starting with the 2006
World Cup in Germany. In the event, Brazil did not perform
at the tournament, going out in the quarter-finals against
France, and Robinho did not meet the expectations placed
upon him. Consequently the English documentary was not
made, but Venancio had already carried out his interviews,
and he kept the recordings. One of the interviews was with
a twelve-year-old Neymar Jr.

A close-up shot of a photo on a wall. In the photo,

Juninho, with his usual red headband and Santos shirt. At his side is Robinho. The interview begins. With his short hair, bare chest and large eyes staring nervously into the camera, Neymar is clearly embarrassed but still confident. He explains that they took the photo the year before, in 2003, when Robinho wanted to get to see him because 'some say I look like him'. Venancio asks Neymar what advice the champion gave him. 'He told me to continue to work hard and study and that one day I would go far.'

'What do you want to do if you make it as a professional footballer and earn lots of money?' the youngster is asked.

'Help my family,' is Neymar's immediate response.

They go past the trophies, the framed newspaper cuttings and the golden boots for best futsal player of 2002 hanging on the wall, an award that Robinho also once won. Neymar mostly answers with 'yes' or 'no' but he wants to let us know that the trophies and cups he has won were because he was a goalscorer; that he did not get angry when the coach took him off the pitch; and that in his brief career he had only been sent off once, for pushing another player. The interviewer changes tack and asks about music. Neymar is not a big fan of music.

Venancio asks why and Neymar admits that he does listen to samba and pagode and that his favourite bands are Revelação and Sorriso Maroto. He knows the words to some songs but he is not prepared to sing.

He is asked what team he supports. 'Palmeiras,' replies Neymar with no hesitation. 'Why? Because I lived through the time when Palmeiras was always the top team, the period when Evair and Rivaldo were there [1993 to 1999, when the São Paulo club won the Paulista League, the Brasilerão and the Coppe Libertadores].'

It is not the best response for someone coming from

Peixe, but each to their own: Neymar is young. And if there is something that is clear, it is that Neymar has a future career in football. Neymar nods. He would like to become a professional footballer at Santos.

Later on, in another interview, he admits he would like to go to Real Madrid or Barcelona. He dreams of following in the footsteps of Pelé and Robinho. His ambition is there for all to see.

Chapter 11

Showtime

A conversation with Robson de Souza, aka Robinho

It is the day before the match against Sampdoria at San Siro. The *Rossoneri* are training at Milanello, the sports complex 50 kilometres outside the capital of Lombardy.

Training finishes just after 6.30pm. After the warm-up there was reflex training, ball possession exercises and the usual friendly match between the first team and the reserves. This is followed by a shower and massage before dinner. Robson da Souza, better known as Robinho, is to start the match.

Robinho, the boy from São Vicente who was called *Neguinho do Chemi* ('little black cemetery guy') when he was little because between one match and another he worked as an unofficial car park attendant at the cemetery in the Bitaru district, arrived at AC Milan on 31 August 2010. Before that he had been back and forth between Europe and Brazil: from Santos to Real Madrid in July 2005, in a transfer worth €30 million, reflecting his then-status as 'the new Pelé'. Three years later, he moved to Manchester City for €42 million. From City he went on loan back to Santos for the 2010 season; then back to Europe, and Manchester City, before being transferred to Milan for €18 million.

In the summer of 2013 it looked as though Robinho was about to go back to Brazil, to Santos, to replace Neymar, but in the end it did not happen. He remained with Massimiliano Allegri's team and renewed his contract until June 2016.

He does not often give interviews but in order to give his view of his friend, Neymar, he is willing to make an exception.

What does it feel like to have been Neymar's idol?
'I am very proud to know that I was the inspiration for a star, a showman like Neymar. Knowing that when he played futsal he said he wanted to be like me and follow in my footsteps makes me very happy.'

When did you meet him?
'I have known Neymar since he was a little boy because I was lucky enough to have the same coach: O Betinho, someone who helped me a lot when I was a kid. The first time I saw him play was when he was nine. I was at Santos and Betinho told me every day, "Come and see this kid, you really must see it for yourself. He looks a lot like you; he is thin like you were at that age and he has the same one-two pass as you. He is amazing, really. Find the time." I played in the first team and what with training sessions and matches I could never find the time. In the end, though, I managed to go and see him play. I fell in love immediately.'

Why?
'He was different to the other kids. He did stuff that was just incredible for a nine-year-old. He had *ginga*, he kicked the ball with both feet, he dribbled in such a tight space that you could not work out how he did it. When I saw him and I saw his technique, I said to myself that this kid would definitely become a star, even if you can never see into the future. He played for Gremetal at the time. It was easy to recognise him

as he wore the headband with "Jesus 100 per cent" on it. If I am not mistaken, it was a match against Corinthians. He took the ball, he made a one-two, then another and another and then when the keeper came out he lobbed it into the net. He scored three goals and one was a real screamer: one touch to flick it over one player and then a volley into the far corner.'

Betinho always said that Neymar looked like Robinho for his one-two pass, his dribbling, his style, his flair at futsal. He was not the only one to have thought this. Do you have a lot in common?

'The way we play, the desire to create a show, to have the ball at our feet is what we have in common. That said, everyone has their own style. Neymar is more of an all-rounder than I am. He scores more goals than I do. When I started in futsal, I had the same capacity to make one-two passes, to dribble, but I was not a finisher like he is. In my first season, I scored ten goals; he scored an incredible 20 or 30.'

In 2006 Neymar went to Spain for a trial with Real Madrid. You were there playing for the 'Galacticos'.

'Yes. I have not forgotten it. I invited him to my house and when he saw there was the *feijoada* [a typical Brazilian dish made with beans, pork, beef and spices, served on a bed of white rice and *farofa*] on the table, he almost started to cry. He said, 'Thank God you are at Madrid.'

In 2010, you went back to Santos for a 20-match spell and together with Neymar you won the Paulista League and the Brazil Cup. You were on the pitch when the boy from Gremetal played for the national team. What was it like playing with Neymar?

Robinho smiles. 'Easy. He is a player that moves well; he knows how to open up spaces and look for goalscoring opportunities. On the pitch, he is a synonym for showtime. I hope I can play with him again, maybe in the national team. At that time, Neymar and I were good friends and we played well together. We took our friendship and happiness off the pitch on to the pitch. We always respected our opponents but we wanted to win and score goals. We were always talking about how we would celebrate goals. Before the match, in the changing rooms, we would agree the celebrations. Our inspiration could have been a new song, an event or a friend to whom we wanted to dedicate the goal. We made up dance routines: from the 'statue of liberty' to the funky rhythm dance. Neymar was always very creative. We had a great time training and during the matches. We laughed like mad, we were always smiling. We were only serious when the manager was telling us off. When the team is doing well and you are flying high, all you can do is enjoy it. It was truly a great year. Happiness was the name of the game for Neymar, for me and for us all. Deep down, us Brazilians are like this.'

You have several years of experience in European football. How do you view Neymar's decision to leave Santos for the Old Continent?
'I spoke to him about it and even though I am a fan of Santos and I would have liked to have seen him still playing in the Peixe shirt, I told him that he had to embark on a new adventure. I told him that, in my view, he would have found something better at Barcelona. Not because I was against Real Madrid but at Madrid the style is different: it is every man for himself.'

How will Neymar adapt to European football?
'It is not easy playing in a different country, playing a different style of football, but I believe Neymar is too intelligent, too good, too quick not to be able to adapt. Barcelona has

a great squad with players like Messi, Iniesta, Xavi, who will no doubt help him. They will make sure that his involvement in the moves and team play is as smooth and as quick as possible. For me, Neymar has gone to the right club in the right country. With Barcelona he will score many goals and win many trophies.'

Do you think he will become an idol here like he is in Brazil?
'I can only say that my son, Robson Junior, who is five and plays futsal, says to me every day that when he is older he wants to be like Neymar. One morning after an away game I got home and Vivian, my wife, said to me, "Guess what Junior did yesterday?" I replied, looking concerned, "What did he do?" She said, "Go and see him." I went into his room and there he was with a 'Neymar' haircut: mohican style. I took a photo and sent it to Neymar. He called me and just started laughing. I told him that it was all his fault that these kids do such stupid things.'

Chapter 12

Madrid

Madrid Football Federation
05/06 season. Youth league
Player registration card application

Sporting name: Neymar
Name: Neymar
First surname: Da Silva
Second surname: Santos Junior
Address: Castillo de Alarcon, 49
City: Villafranca del Castillo
Province: Madrid
Birth place: Mogi das Cruzes
Date of birth: 5.02.92
Country: Brazil
Nationality: Brazilian
Club: Real Madrid CF
Located in: Madrid
Date: 29.03.2006

A yellow card with a photo of a smiling Neymar Jr: this is
the Madrid Football Federation application form of the boy
from Mogi das Cruzes to play for Real Madrid. The form
was authorised on 30 March 2006. This document, taken
from the Federation's archives and published on the front
page of *As*, a Madrid sports daily newspaper, is confirmation
that Neymar Jr, at barely fourteen years of age, could have

been playing for Madrid. It could have been akin to the story of Leo Messi, who moved to Barcelona at thirteen from Newell's in Rosario to then develop at the Catalans' La Masia school. But for Neymar things were to be a bit different.

In March 2006, Neymar Jr took off from São Paulo airport for Madrid. He was accompanied on his first flight by his father and Wagner Ribeiro, his agent, the man who in 2005 sealed Robinho's transfer from Santos to Real Madrid after long and drawn-out negotiations. Ribeiro was introduced to Neymar Pai by Betinho. He was convinced of the talent of Neymar Jr right from the outset and gave the family a monthly income to help them out: he was willing to take a gamble on Neymar Jr, right from when the star was only twelve. Together with Juan Finger, the talent scout famous worldwide for having helped the likes of Maradona, Gullit, Sócrates, Dunga, Klinsmann and Kaká, and also for his run-ins with the Brazilian justice system, Ribeiro managed Neymar's entire early career. He was in the bad books of the Santos management for the Robinho deal but thanks to his contacts with Real Madrid, forged the summer before, he was able to get Neymar a trial with the Spanish giants.

Neymar stayed there three weeks. He was put up in the Colegio Internacional SEK-El Castillo in Villafranca del Castillo, a complex located about twenty kilometres from the capital. It is here where the up and coming Madrid talents live and study. The club made cars available for him so that he and his father could get around and get to know Real Madrid's many sports complexes.

The medicals went well and his first trial impressed the Madrid coaching team. Jesús Gutierrez, who trained the *Infantil A* (youth 'A' team), where the kids were fourteen, was struck by Neymar's quality from the first moment: 'He had tremendous quality. He was a lot better than the other

players at that stage.' And these were not your average footballers: there was Dani Carvajal, now playing for the Real first
team, Pablo Sarabia, now at Getafe, Alex Fernández, now at
Espanyol, Fran Sol, now at Real Oviedo. Neymar was a clear
star. Gutierrez continues, 'Everyone agreed. All the members
of the management team agreed to sign him, and even our
players. Normally when a new player arrives in a group that
has already been formed, there is jealousy and politics. The
first thing the players say is, "This kid is not as good as they
say he is." This time they said, "Coach, this kid is incredible,
he is awesome."'

Neymar played well and in the training matches he
scored a lot of goals: as many as 27 by some accounts. It
looked as though he had fitted easily into the group and
was happy to be in Madrid. He would later say of Real in an
ESPN interview: 'It seemed like a dream and yet Real was a
reality.' Neymar was clearly emotional. He had met his idols:
Ronaldo 'O Fenómeno', Zinedine Zidane, Julio Baptista and
Robinho.

On Sunday 26 March 2005, he was invited to Santiago
Bernabéu to watch a *Liga* match: Real Madrid *vs.* Deportivo
La Coruña. Sitting in the VIP box beneath the chairman of
Real Madrid, he saw the Whites win 4–0 courtesy of goals
from Hector, Ronaldo, Sergio Ramos and Julio Baptista. At
the end of the match Júlio Gomes, Spanish correspondent
for TV Bandeirantes, interviewed him. 'Did you enjoy that?'
he asked. Neymar, smiling, replied, 'Seeing Zidane and
Robinho play … how could that not appeal to me?' He also
said that he liked the city and wanted to stay there.

Wagner Ribeiro then stepped in: 'Neymar came here to
get to know the reality of Madrid so his father could move
to Europe and Neymar could become a great footballer in
Spain, England or Italy; it is just a matter of time. He is a

real talent.' How did Neymar respond to this? 'I don't know anything, it is those two [Ribeiro and his father] who know everything. I just play football.'

After a few days, Real Madrid had reached their decision. The contract was drawn up and agreed by the parties. It had a term of five years. Among the various conditions were a guaranteed job for Neymar's father, appearance bonuses for Neymar and his and his sister's schooling paid for. Just Neymar's mother's signature was missing. Nadine had a plane ticket for Spain but preferred to stay home with Rafaela. Madrid wanted to sign Neymar up in time for the last few matches of the season. Some say that the new recruit was meant to play in a tournament in which the *Infantil A* were taking part a few days later, in Barcelona. But Neymar was not part of the group. He returned to Brazil.

Why?

Because the deal with Real Madrid was not signed. The reasons why do not always match up. Neymar Pai said it was *saudade*, Portuguese for 'nostalgia'. He said that 'Juninho' was getting sadder each day that went by; he had lost his natural happiness; he missed his family, his friends, his city, Santos and even the rice and *feijoada*.

Basically, Neymar Pai claimed that they went back because Neymar Jr followed his heart, even though it is not easy to say no to a new life and a large sum of money. Many criticised his choice: they said he was mad to refuse an offer from one of the most prestigious clubs in Europe; commentators said he had missed the chance of a lifetime. But Neymar Pai was convinced he was acting in the best interests of his son. Money can't buy happiness, as they say. Happiness for the da Silva family was in Santos.

Madrid did not report the matter in exactly the same way. Allegedly the terms were virtually agreed when Wagner

Ribeiro asked for a further €60,000 to close the deal. The sports management of the club agreed. The amount was not over the top. It was achievable. Ramon Martinez, technical secretary for the club, approved the deal and requested that it be completed as soon as possible. But a few of the club officials did not agree. One of them said, 'We are not paying a penny more for a fourteen-year-old kid from Brazil with his whole family in tow.' The identity of the naysayer was not revealed.

It is worth noting that at this time (March 2006) Real Madrid was going through a difficult time in terms of the running of the club. Florentino Perez, the chairman, who had initiated the 'Galacticos' era for the club, had resigned on 27 February that year. He was disappointed with the players that he said he had spoilt rotten and was leaving so that the dynamics and the results of the club could change. In his place came Fernando Martín, a building tycoon, who would act as interim chairman until the elections in June 2006. Martín, though, would leave his office as chairman before the expiry of the mandate. On 26 April 2006, barely two months after having accepted the position, he would hand over to Luis Gómez-Montejano, who was to manage the election process. In short, there was a great deal of uncertainty behind the scenes at the club at this time. And the unclear signals coming from the club's management meant that the deal with Neymar was not achieved, for the sake of the modest sum of €60,000.

Marcelo Teixeira, the then chairman of Santos, does not agree with this version of events: 'Once we heard about the deal with Real Madrid, we moved quickly and called Neymar's parents straight away. We offered Neymar a five-year contract, a pay increase and that we would provide for his family. The father and son wanted to stay in Brazil and, even before Neymar had his successes with Peixe, we had mapped out a career and professional terms and conditions.'

But that was not all. According to Teixeira, Santos contacted the lawyer Marcus Motta, who informed FIFA and the relevant authorities of Real's approach to Neymar Jr – which was not strictly by the book as Neymar was underage. In short, the ex-chairman claims it was his club that won the battle with Real and not that Real Madrid backed out over the extra €60,000.

This may be true, except for one missing detail. According to Neymar Pai, he and Wagner Ribeiro spoke to Zito and Wanderlei Luxemburgo, the then coach at Santos (and ex-coach at Real Madrid). O Pai and Ribeiro called Luxemburgo and asked him to convince the Santos chairman to back young Neymar. At any event, on Juninho's return from Madrid, the meeting held at the University of Santa Cecilia in Santos between his father, his agent and Santos's chairman was successful.

Neymar Jr and his father, at Jardim Gloria in Praia Grande, signed the contract in Zito's presence. One million reais (€400,000) and a salary of 10,000 reais per month meant that Neymar Jr remained at Santos. With so much money, his family could afford to buy a flat opposite Vila Belmiro, and they left Praia Grande.

This is the official version, although how the deal was reached is not clear.

And the story was not over. Indeed it would run and run; so much so that, on 30 August 2007, *UOL Esporte* wrote an article that the young Neymar (by then fifteen) was about to sign a contract with Real Madrid that would have locked him in until 2011. Emilio Butragueño, sports director at Madrid, was convinced that the deal would be signed within a week. Santos would not be due any compensation for the transfer, as they only had a letter of intent signed by Neymar in which the parties agreed to sign a professional contract when Neymar reached sixteen. Wagner Ribeiro said that the final decision was down to the father and son, and that Madrid had a long-term project for Neymar like the ones that made Messi a success at Barcelona and Cesc Fàbregas at Arsenal.

On 13 September 2007, the matter was resolved: the contract for exploitation of Neymar's image, which he had signed with Santos, was extended; the essential terms of Neymar's professional contract were laid down and the break clause for $25 million was inserted.

Neymar Pai commented to ESPN Brasil, 'We are all happy to have reached an agreement. The important thing is that Juninho can relax and play without external pressures.'

Chapter 13

A Copinha

It had just struck five in the afternoon in São Paulo. It was 10 January 2008 and in the Nicolau Alayon stadium, better known as Comendador Sousa, to the west of the megalopolis, a youth football match of the Copa São Paulo was being played.

'La Copinha' is the most important youth tournament in Brazil. It was created to commemorate the anniversary of the founding of the city. The first tournament was held in 1969 and since then many talents have emerged from it: Roberto Falcão, Toninho Cerezo, Raí, Walter Casagrande, Kaká and Robinho.

The 2008 edition, which started on 5 January and ended on 25 January, featured 88 teams split into 22 groups. All of the country's states were represented, even if the majority of the teams (38) were from the state of São Paulo. Nowadays the tournament is reserved for under-17s but in 2008 it was up to the age of twenty.

Neymar Jr was aged fifteen years and eleven months. He was 1.66m (5ft 5in) tall and weighed about 50kg (7st 12lb). On 10 January, he played Santos's second match. They called him up at the last minute to give him some experience, playing against players who were three to four years older than him and clearly taller and more experienced.

The match was broadcast live on Sport TV. Jota Junior, a TV commentator, explained that the greatest hope for the Santos fans was on the bench: a kid whom everyone wanted to see burst on to the pitch as soon as possible. Thirty minutes into the second half, the linesman raised cards to indicate two substitutions: number 10 on one team and number 21 on the other. Neymar jigged up and down on the spot, waiting for Paulo Henrique, the future Ganso, to leave the pitch.

Peixe were winning 3–0 against Barra do Garças, a team from Mato Grosso: a comfortable scoreline, which enabled the coach to take a risk and try out 'Juninho'. A quick handshake and pat on the shoulder from the eighteen-year-old Ganso, the undisputed centre midfielder, and Neymar, number 21, was into the action, taking up a position just behind the centre forwards.

Jota Junior spelt out the age and place of birth of the young Neymar. Another commentator wondered if he was the youngest player of the tournament. Two minutes went by and Neymar was already in action. Square on to the area, he showed some nifty footwork and played an inch-perfect pass to Thiago Luiz, who was unmarked in the area near the penalty spot. The goalie parried the shot but the linesman had already flagged for offside. Number 21 looked at the referee with an inquisitive expression.

Into the 82nd minute: Carleto, on the right, played the ball to Serginho. He played a quick pass to Neymar in the area, who flicked it back. Two paces from the goal, a blue and yellow defender made the clearance.

The 86th minute: Juninho, on the edge of the area, hit a lobbed pass over the defenders to find Vinicius, but the offside flag was up. 'A sensational pass, deft footwork with the ball glued to his foot. There was no way that was offside – a complete injustice,' opined the TV commentator. One minute later, an assist from Juninho and another goal for

Santos. A long pass by the opposing team's goalkeeper; the Santos defence pushed out; Neymar, in his own half, headed the ball on to be picked up by Alemão, who cut into the area and struck the ball goalwards. The Barra do Garças keeper could not hold it. 4–0. Neymar ran over and hugged him and jumped on his back.

It was not over. The players from Mato Grosso scored a consolation goal and feebly celebrated. The reaction was immediate. Neymar on the left darted into the area, skimmed past a player and made an assist: a curving cross to Thiago Luiz, who just slotted it in. 5–1 the final score.

In fifteen minutes the rising star of *Alvinegro* had amazed the crowd and confirmed the hype that had been building about him. He was interviewed at the side of the pitch. They asked him what it was like to play for the first time in the *Copa*; how did he feel knowing that the match was broadcast live, and playing at such an important venue. 'When the match is on TV you get goose bumps,' he replied, 'but when I touched the ball, all my fears disappeared in a flash. Thanks be to God that we played a brilliant match. We are working towards becoming champions.' One commentator continued by saying that the only thing missing was that Neymar did not score. Juninho laughed and said, 'Let's see next time.'

That goal – a penalty – did indeed come on his second appearance, against Nacional of São Paulo. It was a shame that Santos's run ended in the quarter-finals, exiting to Internacional of Porto Alegre on penalties.

Márcio Fernández was the coach of that under-20s team. Nowadays he is coach at Shanghai Shenhua, a Chinese team which bought Nicolas Anelka in 2011 and Didier Drogba in 2012. He remembers that they used to say he was mad for playing a fifteen-year-old with a group of eighteen-year-olds:

'At first, it created a few issues at the club. Then, once people saw him play those amazing matches, they told me off for not having played him sooner. It is true that he skipped a category by coming to play for us but I wanted him to cut his losses and play in a tournament that is important for the development of young players. I put him up against bigger and more experienced players to see how he would react. He clearly showed he was up to the challenge.'

Lino Martins, who was Neymar's coach from age sixteen to seventeen, agrees. He is a friend of Neymar Pai and had known Neymar Jr from when he was a boy playing at Tumiaru and Gremetal. In a hotel bar in Santos, he tells me how he took him from Lima 'at a critical age, an age when you can see whether a kid is going to make it, if he will become a professional.'

'Neymar was different from the others,' says Lino. 'He was still developing, but he had impressive technical skills. He was faster than most players I had seen before. He played a good season in the Paulista league and a good Brasilerão. He scored loads of goals. He had charm and a strong personality. His head was well and truly on his shoulders. It is not easy at that age. If you are good with a ball at that age, you think you are a star, the best in the world, everyone like that goes through it but some lose their way. Neymar did not. I believe that O Pai channelled him very well. As an ex-footballer he knew what the risks and issues of the trade were. He knew that it is not just the footballing ability that counts but also being humble, disciplined, well behaved and with a positive spirit on the pitch. And above all, the hard work day after day.'

After one year, Lino handed his charge over to another coach. Neymar was now in the *Júniores* team, in preparation for the first team.

At the beginning of 2009, he again played in the *Copinha* in São Paulo, but this time from the start. He wore number 7 on his shirt. In the group stages, he scored Santos's third goal against Cene. A foul on the edge of the area gave Santos a free kick and Neymar took it. The position was not the best. Whether he wanted to or not, he had to take it with his left foot. It was not his favoured foot but the ball swerved beautifully through the air and past the wall and smashed into the inside of the right goalpost. Goal!

Santos got through the group stages on maximum points. In the last 32, they met Guarani. The *pequiño* ('little one'), as the TV commentator called him, was the first to score: a header, connecting with a corner taken from the left. Then he headed off to the stands and made up a celebration samba move. And that was not all: the number 7 also finished off the match in style. Chasing a long ball, he ran half the length of the pitch and dummied the keeper for 4–0.

Peixe were through to the last sixteen, where they were to face Cruzeiro. But a 2–1 win for the Belo Horizonte team saw Neymar and his teammates depart the tournament.

Straight after the match, the team started talking about moving Neymar to the first team. Márcio Fernández had been coach since the summer of 2008. He had often let Neymar train with the older players at the CT Rei Pelé. The coach liked to work with three teams on the pitch; a system called *treino alemão* ('German training'). The junior players were required to possess speed and ball control. Neymar had passed the new arrivals test with flying colours. Kléber Pereira, a 33-year-old centre forward who had the most experience in the group, came over and gave him what for – these were the tactics used by the older players to scare the novices and make them understand that professional football is not plain sailing. But the number 7 from the Under 20s team was not intimidated. He fitted in quickly and did one of his usual tricks. A few days before a match against Palmeiras, he convinced his teammates, the group who played in yellow bibs at training, to turn up to the training ground with a plaster over their mouths: a gag, to convey the message that they would no longer dare to say anything against the 'referee' in the friendly matches, namely Serginho Chulapa, a Santos idol of the 1980s.

And yet, even though Neymar fitted in very quickly and was part of the group, even though he trained hard, and notwithstanding that he was expected to play for the first team, Márcio Fernández preferred to go slowly. He was convinced that Neymar was a great player but also believed that he needed experience and a bulkier physique. At seventeen, he did not want the young man overloaded with responsibility. He stated, 'I put him in the reserve first team so that he could get experience and see what professional life was like. There was still time before moving to the first team. The fans must be patient.'

Soon he would call him up to the first team, but he did not want to set a date. On 12 February 2009, Neymar travelled with the team, which was playing against Marilia in a Paulista league match, but he did not play. Santos were beaten 1–0 and Márcio Fernández was forced to resign. 'I thought he was going to play in that match. I did not play him and I regret that,' commented Fernández a few weeks later; by which time Neymar had started to play for the first team.

Chapter 14
Pacaembu

There had never been anything like it in the history of Santos Football Club. Or at least no one can remember a player who received as many standing ovations even before he got on the pitch, the euphoric fans chanting for the seventeen-year-old to be sent on.

It was Saturday 7 March 2009 at Pacaembu, São Paulo's municipal stadium. Santos were playing in the Paulista league against Oeste from Itápolis. The 22,000 paying supporters were mostly Peixe fans.

The match started at 6.30pm and immediately the fans started chanting for Neymar to be sent into battle. Vágner Mancini, the coach who had taken over the team on 14 February following Márcio Fernández's resignation, resisted until thirteen minutes into the second half. He whispered a final few instructions and, two minutes later, sent him on. Neymar strode on to the pitch wearing the black and white shirt, with number 18 on his back. He substituted Mauricio Molina, a Colombian midfielder. A huge roar boomed around the stadium. The moment Neymar Jr, and the fans, had been waiting for had finally arrived.

On the right of the area, Neymar dribbled around one player and then released a missile which hit the cross-bar and the post, narrowly missing the goal. This was his first involvement. It could scarcely have been a better start for the boy from Mogi das Cruzes. At the end of the match (which finished 2–1 to Santos), the number 18 jogged off the pitch to a round of applause. He headed off to play football with his friends. He had made his first appearance and helped the team, who had been unable to break the deadlock in the first half, to win. He did not let anyone down. It was a debut that Vágner Mancini remembers fondly.

Today Mancini is 46 years old. The coach, of Italian descent, now works for Atlético Paranaense. From Curitiba, before lunch and after training, he recalls his time at Santos, when he strung together a series of good results and gave the number 18 his chance to shine:

'When I arrived at Peixe, Neymar was already in the first reserve team but he had not had chance to play. At that time, Santos had players with a lot of experience, but the results were not there. In order for the club to progress, it needed to renew itself.

'The young Neymar had showed me what he was capable of doing in the training sessions. However, lots of people said he wasn't ready and that he should wait another year before moving to the next level. Everyone treated him as a prized jewel, a diamond which needed carefully looking after; something which needed to be cared for and which could not be ruined or broken. I went against the grain a bit: I did not agree with the general opinion of the club because, put simply, I thought he was ready to play.

'I gave him his debut at Pacaembu. All the Santos fans eagerly awaited the arrival of Neymar on the pitch because he had shown such promise right from the under-17s to the under-20s. The expectation which he had created was truly incredible. Everyone wanted to see him on the pitch; they hoped he was the heir to Robinho and Diego.

'I cannot take much credit. I did not launch his career – he did. I gave him an opportunity and Neymar immediately showed he was something special right from the off. His arrival was very convincing. He quickly gained a permanent place in the first team due to his speed and skill levels. The fans instantly fell in love with him. Not just for his delightful football. Neymar was charismatic and likable. He was someone who you immediately connected with. Behind the athlete and the talented footballer, you saw the human element: humble, straightforward and kind – things which are very important for a star. A quality which he has not lost to this day.'

What does a coach say to a young lad who is about to make his career debut?

'I asked him if he was ready to go on. For a seventeen-year-old, his reply was more than convincing. He said he was absolutely ready for this moment, which he had been building up to for a long time, and that he did not feel the pressure. My instructions were simple, those of anyone who has to deal with kids. I told him to believe in himself and not to be afraid to dribble, go for goal and play like he knew how. And he did it. He did not get scared or intimidated by the stage he was playing on.'

Nor has Mancini forgotten Neymar's great joy when he scored his first goal, eight days after his debut. It was Sunday evening, 15 March 2009. Neymar had played his first home match on 11 March at Vila Belmiro against Paulista. In the second half he replaced Domingos, the central defender, and he had given it his all: dribbling here and there, one-two passes, lobs, cutting passes, the lot. He had made it really hard for the other team's defence. He even scored but it was ruled out for offside. He smiled at the TV cameras to show how close he had come but it was not to be.

He made up for it four days later at Pacaembu. Five first-team players were not match-fit and so Mancini played

Neymar against Mogi Mirim, Rivaldo's old team. Neymar wore the number 7 shirt and in the seventeenth minute he got his first chance. He skipped around a defender and shot. Marcelo Cruz, the Mogi goalkeeper, blocked it. In the 35th minute, Paulo Henrique launched the ball upfield and dashed forward but the ball rebounded off defender Julio Cesar. The stalemate was only broken in the second half. Paulo Henrique scored in the eleventh minute and Ron in the 23rd. Santos were ahead 2–0. They kept the pressure on and five minutes later, in the 28th minute, Neymar scored his first goal.

The move started way back. Molina pushed past the half-way line and passed to Germano, who saw an opening on the left and passed to Triguinho, who in turn darted into the area and crossed it into the centre. Neymar burst forward from nowhere and with a diving header scored his first goal.

It was 6.37pm and Santos were 3–0 up. Neymar raised his index finger aloft and jumped in the air, punching the sky. He imitated the gesture of his greatest idol: Pelé. Neymar commented at the end of the match, 'I wanted to celebrate that way because I had promised my father I would do so.'

It was dedicated to Ilzemar, his grandfather, a huge fan of Pelé. It was Ilzemar who had shown him so many videos of O Rei's goals, who had accompanied him to the park and, while Neymar's cousins played with their dolls, kicked the ball around with 'Juninho'. Ilzemar, the father of Neymar Pai, died in 2008 without being able to see his grandson play for Santos. Now here was a tribute to the memory of his grandfather and a way to please his father.

After jumping to the sky, the young kid from Mogi went to hug Paulo Henrique, his friend and teammate from the Under-20s. All of this while the commentator for Sport TV, Milton Leite, announced, 'The kid from Santos shines!

This is an historic goal right here! This is an historic date for Brazilian football!'

Mancini brought the number 7 off and the fans roared. Neymar came back on at the end of the match to hug one of his opponents: the striker, Giovanni, who had been the idol of the Santos fans at the beginning of the 1990s before going on to play for Barcelona between 1996 and 1999. Neymar talked to the TV journalists and said that he was hoping to be playing the following Sunday in the match against Corinthians, for whom one of his idols played: Ronaldo Luís Nazário da Lima – 'O Fenómeno'.

In the stands, the fans were ecstatic. Many had come to see Neymar and the kid did not disappoint. 'He must play', 'He must start the match', 'He is the best player we've seen since Robinho and Diego', 'He has shown his maturity and his talent' were among the opinions from the crowd. The TV commentators also chimed in. Glenda Kozlowski, former athlete turned presenter and journalist, was the most enthusiastic. She predicted, 'Neymar could be the future Pelé.'

The young star continued to score goals. At Vila Belmiro against Rio Branco in the Brazil Cup he scored his second. This time he had agreed the choreography of the celebrations with his teammates. For his third goal, he invented a new dance, with Madson and Rodrigo Souto getting in on the act. This was a scorcher of a goal, scored on 11 April 2009 against Palmeiras in the first leg of the Paulista League semi-final, to give Santos a 2–1 lead to take into the second leg. Neymar received the ball on the edge of the box. He brought it under control and skipped and danced around his opponents and then let rip with his right foot. The ball shot through a defender's legs and slotted into the corner. Peixe won the second leg with the same result and reached the final. But against Ronaldo's Corinthians, there was no chance. At Vila Belmiro, O Fenómeno, who had come back from Europe (PSV Eindhoven, Barcelona, Internazionale, Real Madrid and Milan), scored two fantastic goals in a 3–1 first-leg victory for his team. This meant that on 3 May at Pacaembu, Corinthians needed only a draw to win their 26th Paulista League title.

After fifteen years in Europe, Ronaldo took home his second Brazilian league title. (His first was in 1994 when he won the Mineiro League with Cruzeiro.) Ronaldo was awarded best player, while Neymar Jr won the award for revelation of the year. Mancini remarked, 'He deserved it. In those two months, in those few matches, he showed great maturity, so much so that at the start of the *Brasileirão* [the national league championship, which takes place in the second half of the season] he was one of the most important players in the team.'

It was a shame that the national league campaign was to mark the end of Mancini's time at Santos. On 13 July 2009, after a terrible defeat (6–2) by Vitória at Salvador de Bahia, he was sacked by chairman Marcelo Teixeira. In his place came Vanderlei Luxemburgo, who had coached Santos on several previous occasions: 1997–98, 2004, and 2006–07. With Peixe he had won one Paulista league, one Brasileiro league and one Rio–São Paulo tournament.

On 20 July, the day when he was officially presented to the club, he said that his aim was to take Santos to where it should be, among the elite of Brazilian football. He would, he said, move Santos up from fourteenth in the table. Vanderlei's first match in the dugout was against Atlético Paranaense. Neymar came on in the second half and immediately changed the rhythm of the game. He scored the winning goal with a screamer, to save the new coach from a poor start.

On 8 August, after a draw at Vila Belmiro against Avai of Florianópolis, the manager reflected on the great joy he had had working with the youth teams. When asked why Neymar was not in the starting line-up (in the first five matches under his rule, Neymar had started only once, against Flamengo), Vanderlei remarked, 'This year, everyone has been telling me that Neymar is one of the best. At some point, he will be a top-level footballer, but I am convinced that he was introduced to the first team too early. He should have played at the lower levels for longer so he could have matured. You need to be patient with him, you need to prepare him for this commitment. He is a *filé de borboleta* ['stick insect']. He is little and cannot withstand the physical contact of a match. He looks like Robinho when he started. He needs to build up his muscle mass. I do not want to burn him out.'

This meant that under Luxemburgo's reign, Neymar was almost always on the bench. He had to go on a hypercalorific diet with meals every three hours in order to gain strength and build 3kg of muscle mass. He needed to do this, according to the technical staff, so that he could play at the top level. It was a difficult time for the seventeen-year-old who, only a few months earlier, had signed a dream five-year contract with Santos (expiring in 2014): 80,000 reais a month and a break clause of 90 million reais.

Club officials were worried. They were concerned that after 31 matches and eight goals, the star would not develop further, either from a physical or a footballing perspective.

Neymar did not like being the 'stick insect'. He thought Vanderlei was having a joke but he wanted to get rid of this nickname as soon as possible.

Chapter 15

Baroque and minimalism

*A conversation with Eduardo Gonçalves
de Andrade, aka Tostão*

'Last Sunday was a special day. I saw seventeen-year-old Neymar's first match, where he played from the start, for Santos. I was so excited, like when I saw Zico, Ronaldo, Ronaldinho and Romário play for the first time.'

The author of these four lines was Tostão. Three days had passed since 'Juninho's' first goal against Mogi Mirim, and one of the greatest critics of Brazilian football, writing for *Folha de S. Paulo* (a Brazilian newspaper) had no doubts when stating, 'We are in the presence of a future star, not just an excellent footballer.'

He stated that Neymar's touch was 'beautiful, efficient and natural', i.e. that of a player in a different league. He continued by saying that Neymar should have more faith in his abilities, be more ambitious and want to be number one. He advised him to become a warrior, someone who did not hide, who got stronger in the face of adversity and who sweated blood and tears.

Eduardo Gonçalves de Andrade, better known as Tostão, class of 1947, was one of the greats in the history of Brazilian football: the white king who, together with Pelé, Carlos Alberto, Jarzinho and Rivelino won the Mexico 1970 World

Cup, beating the Italy of Gigi Riva, Roberto Boninsegna, Sandro Mazzola and Gianni Rivera 4–1 in the final at the Azteca Stadium. He was a doctor and university professor but after the 1994 World Cup he returned to football as a commentator. Today he is considered one of the most important analysts of the game and its heroes.

From Belo Horizonte where he lives, he talks to me about the opinion he gave about Neymar:

'Yes. It is true. When I saw him play the first few matches with Santos, he made me feel the same way as I had when watching the great Brazilian players at the start of their careers. I was not wrong. That first impression has come true over the years.'

And what is your opinion today?
'I believe that Neymar is a fantastic footballer. I am convinced that, over the next few years, he will certainly be one of the candidates for best footballer in the world.'

What technical abilities do you appreciate in Neymar's play?
'He has almost all the qualities of a great footballer: he dribbles very well and with speed; he changes direction with great agility; he can lead with his left or right foot; he is a good striker of the ball; he is very fast, creative, intelligent and has pinpoint accuracy in finishing both in and outside the box; he is a *goleador* (a top goalscorer); he can score with his left or his right foot, his head, from a free kick; he takes corners well and can bend them into the box. Perhaps the best quality he has, which makes the difference compared to other stars, is his ability to dribble the ball with both legs and to score with both feet – something which I had only seen Pelé do.'

You said that he has 'almost every quality'. What is he missing?
'Maybe he needs to learn to not go down so easily. When Leo Messi starts dribbling and the marker goes in for the tackle, trying to block him with his body, nothing happens. Messi continues to run and dribble, to move forward towards the goal. Neymar, on the other hand, falls over, because he is still a bit weak physically but also because he likes creating a bit of theatre, histrionics, to gain the crowd's attention; you know, he fakes a foul. It is a defect of youth which he is slowly growing out of. Barcelona and European football will help him to correct this aspect of his game. Another thing Neymar needs to improve is his muscle mass. He needs to be a bit stronger without losing his agility, his speed and coordination, which are spectacular.'

What does Neymar represent for Brazil?
'Since 2011 he has been the best Brazilian footballer, without a doubt. We have great players but he is the star. He is the best that Brazilian football can offer today. At the beginning, there was a sort of reluctance, resistance against him, perhaps because of his way of playing on the pitch, but bit by bit he became the key player for Santos and the Brazilian team. Neymar brings together the *jogo bonito* ('beautiful game'), the artistic game, namely skill and creativity with productivity and efficiency. He can be one of the greatest footballers in the history of Brazilian football.'

What did he mean to Santos?
'He was fundamental in rekindling the glories of a club in crisis which had not made an impression for over 40 years. But we need to remember that at the beginning of his career, Neymar had a good team around him: Ganso, Robinho, André … but then slowly he was left on his own. They did

not sell him but they sold his teammates and he had to bear the responsibility of the entire team. His performances for Santos got worse. The moment had come that he could no longer play for Santos. It would be like Messi playing in a team in Rosario, Cristiano Ronaldo playing at Madeira and Ibrahimovic playing for a Swedish team. The gap between Neymar and the other players was too big. He was wasting his time and his talent. Fortunately, he moved to an exceptional team, Barcelona, where he could grow and develop next to players like Messi, Xavi and Iniesta. It was a test for him, an important test to understand how far he could go and to allow us to measure his brilliance. Because there are players who shine on their own but when they play with the greats their spark fades.'

You mean the Barcelona stars could have the opposite effect on Neymar?
'It is too early to tell but I am convinced that this will not be the case. I think Barcelona will have two world-class stars in Messi and Neymar. Let's not forget that before Messi, Ronaldinho was Barcelona's golden boy. Messi grew in the shadow of Ronaldinho and then he overtook him as he was a superior player and more of an all-rounder.'

Please could you try and compare Messi, Neymar and Cristiano Ronaldo?
'Messi is extraordinary: he is an incredible dribbler and finisher. Neymar has a greater repertoire but that does not mean he is better. At the moment, Messi is the best player, without a doubt. Cristiano Ronaldo's great quality is his strength. He is a player who has great stamina, a blistering shot on him, great height when heading the ball – but he does not have the skill or magic that Neymar or Messi have.

'Neymar's style is more baroque, more effervescent than

Messi's. Messi is more classic and more technical. Almost minimalist. He uses the least number of moves or touches necessary to create something extraordinary. Neymar is exceptionally theatrical in the way he plays and he is more like Maradona than Messi, but this does not mean he is not effective. Diego liked to show off but it was extremely effective. He loved a spectacle and showing how good he was with a ball. Messi is more like Pelé. Like O Rei, Messi has an incredible ability to get to the crux of a move which Neymar does not have. He would use a few moves to get to a goal-scoring opportunity. I never saw Pelé overdo it with dribbling or waste time dribbling for the sake of it. He flashed past his opponents with the sole aim of getting to the goal. Just like Messi. Pelé's game was pure. Just like a great writer who in a few words says everything there is to be said, whereas others fill pages and pages but say little or nothing.

'A Brazilian who is like an Argentinian and an Argentinian who is like a Brazilian: weird huh? But let's be clear: Neymar is not on a par with Pelé (who was the best) nor Maradona (with his endless repertoire of moves) nor Messi, at least for the time being – even if he could get there in the future.'

He may not be at their level but he is a national icon, and much more than that …
'In Brazil, he is treated like a celebrity and sometimes this can be a problem for him. In Barcelona, he will not be as much of a celebrity, at least for now. And this is definitely a positive thing. He will have more time to train, to rest and to concentrate on football.'

How do you see the number 10 of the Canarinha (Brazilian national team) at the 2014 World Cup?
'Neymar is the great hope, the star of the team. There is

hope that Brazil can win the World Cup in their home country, that they can lift the cup after twelve years. After the victory in the Confederations Cup, Brazil are serious candidates and Neymar is the player that everyone had been waiting for. When he first played in the national team, it did not quite work out; he was on his own too much without support, but now Brazil has settled and developed, Neymar can shine just like he did in the Confederations Cup.'

Chapter 16

Having fun

The music resembles a prelude to a nineteenth century operetta. Then the curtains go back and, on the black background, writing flaps about: 'De Santos FC, para Torcida Santista' (From Santos FC, for the Santos fans). At the back can be seen the pitches of CT Rei Pelé's.

Dressed in a tuxedo, Madson takes off his top hat: 'Ladies and gentlemen ...'

Wearing a black jacket, Neymar moves towards the TV camera: 'We would like to invite all the Santos fans for 17 January ...'

Dorival Junior: '... at the Pacaembu stadium.'

Madson shows the black and white striped shirt: 'Mandatory dress code: the Santos uniform.'

Neymar's turn: 'I would like to present to you the waiter for the evening, Paulo Henrique, O Ganso.'

O Ganso, dressed in evening wear, continues: 'And here we have the main dish: the match between Santos and Rio Branco.'

Neymar: 'We are counting on you being there.'

Paulo Henrique: 'Mark it in your diaries: Sunday, 7.30pm.'

Madson: 'We hope you enjoy the evening.'

He bows and the red curtain closes.

Forty-three seconds of video to invite the fans to the first Peixe match for the 2010 season: the first round of the Paulistão.

In the event it was a beautiful evening, deserving of the

big build-up. There were hugs and kisses between the players after a 4–0 win: two goals for Ganso and two for Neymar.

Neymar was on form and had a new look: Mohican hair. When Neymar Pai saw two red Indians come on to the pitch (his son and André) with the same haircut, he could not believe his eyes. And to think it was he who had asked 'Juninho' to cut his hair. The boy had let it grow long and his father did not like it long, but that he would go ahead and do something like that was unbelievable.

Neymar Jr explained to a horrified Ganso, 'I wanted a change.' Ganso came straight back with 'I am not cutting my hair like that!' To tell the truth, Neymar had already had a similar haircut at the end of 2009 but it was only at the beginning of the season that he found the courage to show it off.

Cosme Salles, Neymar's hairdresser from when Juninho was fifteen, explained, 'He wanted something new so I suggested the Mohican.' Or more correctly, the Mohawk: shaved hair on the sides and a central strip of spiky long hair. It was a cut that became popular at the end of the 1970s thanks to the English punk movement: anarchy, rebellion against the state, against the establishment, and 'no future'. A 'f*** off' attitude to the world with the crest held high.

In Neymar's case, the cut was a lot softer, less aggressive and did not have political or anarchical overtones. It was a question of fashion. Nevertheless it made its mark and became Neymar's brand. Its thousands of variations (more or less gel, coloured, natural, bleached, dreads, completely shaven on the sides or large quiff at the front) were a hit. Twenty cuts over three years struck a chord and spread like wildfire. Babies, kids, fans and players both in and out of Brazil copied the look. It was an enormous success.

One of those who did not like it, along with Neymar Pai, was João Araújo, O Didì, Pelé's barber. His barber shop is right in front of Vila Belmiro. The sign outside the shop, with a Santos crest at either end, reads 'Cabeleireiro de Pelé e de voce tambem' (Hairdresser to Pelé and to you too). The inside of the shop is a football history museum: photos, portraits, autographs, scarves and pennants which date back to 1956 when he cut O Rei's hair for the first time. He explains that 'the Mohican cut in my day was the cut of a *maloqueiro* [an offensive term used in Rio Grande do Sul to define those people living in the shacks and shanties], but I must admit that today it is possible to do a decent Mohican cut.'

Even Didì appreciates the latest fashion up to a point. Especially as Pelé has shown Neymar some photos of when Pelé was seventeen and he did his military service – he jokingly claimed that it was in fact he, Pelé, who launched the Mohican style 50 years earlier, thanks to Didì. If you look at pictures of Pelé at the 1958 World Cup in Sweden, you can see what he means.

Jokes and fashion phenomena aside, Neymar's cut appears to have brought him luck.

The new Peixe coach, Dorival Junior, who had taken over from Luxemburgo, said on 30 December 2009 (the day of his presentation) that he had a group of young players, developed by the club, who could be trusted. Neymar was one of them. And so after the nickname of 'stick insect', the star was back at the forefront again. Dorival Junior used him in an attacking trio with Paulo Henrique Ganso and André, and then integrated Robinho to create an attacking front four who would become known in Brazil as *O Quarteto Santástico* (*Santástico* being a compound of 'Santos' and *fantástico* – 'fantastic').

Robinho, Neymar's idol, had come back from Manchester City, like the prodigal son returning in the Gospel of Luke. He did not get much of a look in at Roberto Mancini's Manchester City and was often on the bench. When he had the option to go on loan to either Benfica or Santos, he did not hesitate for a second.

On 7 February in the Baueri Arena, Robinho, the Santos star from 2002 to 2005, made his second debut in the black and white shirt. He came on twelve minutes into the second half when the score was 1–1. Neymar had scored the first goal, taking his tally to seven for the season: after a foul in the box on Auruca, Neymar had converted the penalty – five steps back, a dummy shot and Rogério Ceni, the goalkeeper for São Paulo, could do nothing but watch the ball hit the back of the net as he dived to the right. Ceni, a player with over 1,000 matches under his belt and, amazingly for a goalkeeper, 100 goals scored – an institution of Brazilian football – was dumbfounded. He gesticulated, saying it was not a *paradinha* but a *paradòn* – not a mere dummy but deception. From Madrid, via Twitter, Kaká agreed and criticised Neymar, saying that only in Brazil could you get away with a fake like that. For Ceni, the goal and the celebratory dance were humiliating, showing a lack of respect by a young player against a veteran. In the years that followed, the two often did not see eye to eye.

The match had continued and Roger had equalised for São Paulo. Then it was time for *O Rei do drible* and *de pedalada*, that is, Robinho, to come to the fore. In the 85th minute, with a flick of the heel he deflected a cross from Wesley at the near post and the ball went in. The daily São Paulo sports paper, *Lance*, reported, 'Robinho showed that he still has a lot to give to football. With an exquisite touch, he guarantees victory to Santos and top of the table in the Paulista league.'

After the 'dress rehearsal', *O Quarteto Sántastico* continued to impress. The match on 10 March 2010 saw Peixe's highest score in the history of the Brazil Cup: Santos 10 Naviraiense 0. Neymar scored the second and the seventh goal, the latter a memorable goal in the 54th minute. He received the ball from Giovanni on the edge of the box. With a series of dummies, he left the two defenders standing, a third soon followed suit and the goalkeeper had no chance. The TV commentators boomed 'Gol de Placa' – an expression alluding to Pelé's great goal on 5 March 1961 against Fluminense, for which a commemorative plaque was put up at Maracana.

This Neymar goal was of no less importance. The best goal in the *Copa do Brasil*, the best of the season claimed the TV commentators. Wait and see ...

At Vila Belmiro, on 14 April 2010 – Santos's 98th birthday – Neymar scored five goals against the Guarani in the last sixteen of the cup.

2nd minute: Penalty converted with a dummy.

30th minute: Missile from his left foot on the edge of the area.

38th minute: On his own in front of goal he slotted in a pass from Arouca.

81st minute: Meeting Robinho's cross from the left, he took two touches and scored.

85th minute: Matsu stormed upfield and passed to Robinho, who flicked to Neymar: goal.

The final score: Santos 8 Guarani 1.

But it was not the avalanche of goals or beautiful play which won fans and followers over. It was the spreading of joy and the desire to have fun which oozed from the pores of the latest generation of *Meninos de la Vila*. This group of players, which harked back to the earlier generations from the 1960s, 1978 and 2002, was *brincadeira* ('fun'), as the Brazilians say.

Each goal was a party with a different jig, something fun and different. In the match against Guarani, they invented one dance after another: the baseball hat and rap, the tennis match, the motorbike, the lorry, the rolling planes, the merry-go-round, the military march, the shoeshiner and the signature dances to music from the movies. The range of dances seemed endless.

On 21 March 2010, in a league match against Ituano, even the Statue of Liberty got a look in.

Neymar was not playing as he was on a one-match ban. He was in New York with Santos B, playing a friendly against the Red Bulls. Before the match he called André and asked him to do something for him and to imitate the Statute of Liberty when they scored. André scored the equalising goal and together with Madson and Wesley he made his way to the edge of the pitch. With his hand held up high as if he were holding the torch, the three made the shape of the Statue of Liberty. When Paulo Henrique scored the second, the image was repeated, much to the amusement of Neymar, who was watching the match on TV. Neymar called his friend straightaway to thank him.

It is worth noting that, even with Neymar out and Robinho injured, the match finished a scandalous 9–1.

'When we won by [only] two or three goals, everyone said Santos was in trouble. We had fun when we played but we played responsibly. The atmosphere in the changing rooms and the stadium was awesome. It was one of the best years of my life,' commented Neymar, years later.

It was a season that brought two league titles to Santos: the first and second of Neymar's career. On 2 May 2010, Pacaembu Stadium was the venue for the away match of the final of the Paulista league. Peixe were there, having beaten their eternal rivals, São Paulo, in the semis: two brilliant victories: 3–2 at Morumbi and 3–0 at home. At Vila Belmiro, Neymar scored the first with a header. Then, from the penalty spot, another dummy. This time a little less obvious but the victim was the same: Rogério Ceni. The final was against

Santo André, another underdog team come good. The first leg at Pacaembu finished 3–2 to Peixe. Neymar was injured and was replaced by André at half-time.

In the second leg, Neymar was on top form. The match was a tough one. Santos's number 11 scored two goals. The first was a real masterpiece: Robinho flicked the ball to Neymar in the area. Neymar beat two defenders and the goalkeeper and fired the ball into the back of the net. The kid from Mogi das Cruzes scored the second as well. He was then substituted for Roberto Brun.

The scoreline now stood at 2–2. Santo André did not give up and took the lead 3–2. With Peixe suffering three red cards, it looked an uphill challenge for Santos, but somehow the eight on the pitch managed to keep the boat afloat. Paulo Henrique was called to the bench but he protested and stayed on. He even managed to invent a tactic never seen before: he moved forward on the left wing but, with no one in the centre and no other player close, he decided to leave the ball on the corner spot and wait for a player on the other team to go and get the ball. He then put the player under pressure, to waste time – when you're three men down, any move is a good move if it wastes a bit of time. The referee finally blew full-time with the score still 3–2, Santos having been behind for much of the match. It levelled the score at 5–5 across the two legs, but Santos won the title based on their superior goal difference in the earlier stages of the competition.

The crowd went wild and the fans were jumping up and down in the stands. It was party time and Neymar, with tears of joy in his eyes, received the Paulista league medal.

After the excitement of winning the great gold cup, disappointment was just around the corner. Even though the fans had shouted 'Neymar for Brazil' many times, and even though Pelé and Zico had been in favour of calling him up for the *Seleção*, Dunga, the Brazilian coach, did not buckle under the pressure: neither Neymar nor Paulo Henrique would be taking part in the 2010 World Cup in South Africa. This was a knock-back for the *Meninos de Vila* who had been on a golden run. So many people wanted to see Neymar play in the World Cup, as Pelé had when he was seventeen and amazed the world in 1958. Juninho would have to wait another four years. Brazil eventually lost in the quarter-finals to Holland. Millions of Brazil fans were in mourning.

Santos relieved the post-World Cup depression by winning the Brazil Cup. The first leg, on 28 July against Vitória at Vila Belmiro, finished 2–0 to Santos. Neymar chested the first off a cross from Pará but then spooned a penalty: the ball ended up in the goalkeeper's hands. Neymar was booed from the stands. Every time he got the ball the crowd teased him, as if to let Neymar know that sometimes his arrogance was too much to take. In the end, despite this mishap, the match finished well. In the return leg at Bahia on 4 August, despite losing 2–1, Santos took the cup. Neymar was the leading goalscorer for the tournament with eleven goals. He also scored fourteen in the Paulistão. He was the undisputed Brazilian idol.

In an interview with *Estado de São Paulo* in April 2010, Neymar told the paper that his dream car would be a yellow Porsche – with a red Ferrari in the garage (even though he had just bought a Volvo XC60 for 140,000 reais). He said he wanted to go to Disneyland because he loved the amusement parks. He collected watches, perfumes and bought designer clothes: Calvin Klein and Armani. He was enrolled on the electoral register but he had no idea who the presidential candidates were. He had not paid much attention to Lula da Silva for the time being, although he swore he would do so in the future. Basically, here was a rich and famous kid who still needed to mature. He would do so sooner than he expected.

Chapter 17

Ayrton Senna

The first offer was a tester. West Ham United offered 15 million at the end of June 2010 for the eighteen-year-old Neymar. The idea was that the Santos striker would play one or two seasons with West Ham before moving to Chelsea. The Hammers were to be the testing ground for the Blues of Roman Abramovich. A neat way to try and pay less for the end product. A similar approach worked well in 2006 with Argentinians Javier Mascherano and Carlos Tevez. Coming from Corinthians, they started at West Ham and then ended up at Liverpool and Manchester United respectively.

The offer was appealing to Neymar Pai. He was convinced that his son could adapt to English football without too much difficulty and go on to become one of the great stars of European football. Santos were not so keen to negotiate. The club, which owned 60 per cent of Neymar's registration (40 per cent was owned by Dis Group, the sports arm of Grupo Sonda, the largest supermarket chain in the state of São Paulo), knew that behind West Ham was Chelsea, and so they wanted to wait for a better offer. In the meantime, Santos reminded the bidders that there was a break clause for €35 million and that it had no intention of underselling Neymar and thus breaking up the team, which in 2010 was a dream team.

A new offer from Chelsea landed a few days later. Abramovich and his partners put €20 million on the table.

On 20 July, Santos issued a press release on its website stating that they were grateful for the interest but were not willing to start negotiations for Neymar at that price. It was horse-trading, which escalated over the following few days. The offer rose to €30 million, with a five-year contract worth €3.5 million per season to Neymar, plus match bonuses, league bonuses and various perks.

It was an offer that the da Silva Santos family could not refuse. At the beginning of August, Neymar Pai and Wagner Ribeiro flew to New York, where Brazil were playing a friendly, with Neymar due to start, to negotiate with Chelsea. Santos remained adamant that they did not want to sell to the English league champions, then managed by Carlo Ancelotti.

In an interview with *Radio Globo*, Wagner Ribeiro stated, 'Luis Álvaro de Oliveira Ribeiro, the Santos chairman, is a decent and honourable man; he has all my respect and that of Neymar's father. Objectively speaking, I think he is a dreamer. Any Brazilian club would love to have an offer like the one from Chelsea. He is the only one to have received an offer that any chairman would want but which was not accepted. It is a shame that contracts have to be honoured.'

Ribeiro had no doubt that it was time for Neymar Jr to leave Brazil. He could not see the need for the young Neymar to stay at Santos. In order to grow and develop, he needed to move. It may even have been counterproductive to stay in Brazil because, as he said, 'in Brazil there are better footballers but the league is not as good. Playing in the Champions League is totally different to any other competition in our country.' In Ribeiro's mind, it was a done deal: 'it was just down to the family now'.

But it was still Santos's move. They needed to make a winning move in a few days. Luis Álvaro de Oliveira Ribeiro called on Armiño Neto, the marketing manager for the club, who he had brought in when he was elected. Ribeiro said, 'I have €30 million on the table but I do not want to sell Neymar: I want to sell the show. We do not have the financial clout to pay the salary that Chelsea is offering. But we need to find the money to keep him here; we need to lay down a new contract, a new deal, but above all offer him and his father a career project. We need to talk about his future.'

In a room in the Hotel Porto Bay in São Paulo, a stone's throw from Avenida Paulista, Neto, the marketing manager, who left Santos in July 2013, runs through the steps of what was called 'Project Neymar'.

The idea was simple: develop the Neymar brand to find a sponsor which would enable the club to match the salary offered by the English. A complicated task because for it to work, Neymar's father, Neymar and his agent all needed to be on board. Neto was to look after the key concepts and the marketing and the chairman was to look after the financing.

On 17 August 2010, at Banco Santander's offices, the decisive meeting was held: a tense and difficult meeting which saw the participation of all the interested parties. Neto thought to himself, 'How do you tell Neymar Pai that his son is special, that he has all the characteristics of a star and could become the most loved player in Brazil? How do you convince him that it would have been a good thing to stay at Santos?'

He thought of other great sportsmen: Pelé, Roger Federer, Maradona and David Beckham. He then put his marketing hat on and thought of an image that could work.

The meeting started at 10.00am. Santos's chairman switched the lights off and pointed at the screen. The first slide of Project Neymar came up. An empty chair. Disbelief echoed around the room. Neymar Pai said, 'What's this …?

The *filé de borboleta* ('stick insect'): seventeen-year-old Neymar Jr celebrates scoring for Santos in a Brazil Cup match in March 2009. (LatinContent/Getty Images)

O Quarteto Santástico: Neymar (number 17) celebrates a goal with teammates Robinho, André and Paulo Henrique. The goals and exuberant attacking play of this quartet defined Santos's successful 2010 season. (Ernesto Rodrigues/Agencia Estado via AP Images)

Santos players celebrate Neymar's goal in the final of the 2011 Copa Libertadores against Peñarol of Uruguay. It proved a crucial strike as the match finished 2–1 to the Brazilian side. (AP Photo/Andre Penner)

Neymar, still a Santos player, comes up against Barcelona in the Club World Cup in Japan, 2011. A 4–0 win for Barça underlined the gulf between Spanish and Brazilian club football and reinforced the notion that Neymar would one day have to move to Europe to make the most of his talent. (AP Photo/Shuji Kajiyama)

Heir to Pelé: for the friendly game against England in June 2013, Brazil coach Luiz Felipe Scolari gave Neymar the iconic number 10 shirt – an indication of the player's talismanic status for the national team. (Getty Images)

Neymar steps on to the Camp Nou pitch for his presentation as a Barcelona player following his mu anticipated trar (Lino de Vallie Demotix)

Brazil celebrate winning the Confederations Cup in July 2013. Their success in the tournament, especially the final victory over world and European champions Spain, led to them being installed as favourites for the 2014 World Cup. (AP Photo/Victor Caivano)

Camp Nou erupts and Barcelona's players congratulate their new teammate (number 11) after his opening goal in a 2–1 win over Real Madrid – a highlight of Neymar's first season in Spain. (AP Photo/Emilio Morenatti)

We are talking about contracts, money. What has an empty chair got to do with anything?'

The chairman explained, 'That is the chair of the great national sports hero. It has remained empty since Ayrton Senna left us. Gustavo Kuerten was about to sit there but due to an injury at only 29 years of age, he had to quit his tennis career. Ronaldo O Fenómeno left for Europe at seventeen years of age. The chair is empty. If your son rejects the offer from Chelsea and stays with Santos, it will be the first step to earning the right to sit in that chair.'

Neto remembered the speech word for word. It had a great impact and was very effective. Those attending the meeting were impressed, including Neymar Pai. It was only the first trump card from Santos. Next came the good and bad points of a career with Santos (including numbers).

At 10.40 the chairman's phone rang. Luis Álvaro de Oliveira Ribeiro gave the phone to an inquisitive-looking Neymar Pai. Who could be calling during such an important meeting? On the other end of the line was Pelé. O Rei spoke and Neymar listened. He told him it was not the time to be leaving Santos to try something new in Europe. Neymar needed to be stronger and more mature and aware of his skills so as to be able to achieve his objectives on the Old Continent. He assured Neymar Pai that if it were his son he would not make such a decision. He reminded Neymar Pai that, even though they were different times, his entire career was spent with Santos and that he won world and national titles with Peixe.

When Neymar Pai got off the phone and gave it back to Luis Álvaro, he was on another planet. His expression was one of a father who had just realised that Santos was also concerned about the well-being of his family.

Neto explained, 'The presentation ended with a short

and emotional statement saying that Neymar would indeed go to Europe but he would go after having won all he could win with Santos and he would leave as an idol for everyone. When Neymar Pai entered the room that day he was 99 per cent convinced he was going to sign with Chelsea but after the meeting he was in two minds. He asked for some time to think and to speak to his family. At 5.00pm a meeting was set up in Ribeiro's offices. As soon as I saw Neymar Pai, I knew that Neymar Jr was going to stay with Santos.'

On 19 August the final decision was made public. Neymar Jr had signed a new five-year contract with Santos with a break clause of €45 million. His salary had gone up from 170,000 to 600,000 reais a month. Other than Ronaldo, who was on 1,000,000 reais a month with Corinthian, Neymar was the highest-paid player in Brazil. And that was not all: the new contract envisaged that Neymar would receive a significant portion of the earnings from his image and a bonus if he was selected for the national team.

The chairman and Neymar Jr held a press conference to explain the details of the deal. A beaming Neymar Jr confirmed that he had taken on board the advice of many but in the end it was his decision and his decision alone. He was happy to be able to continue playing for Santos. Luis Álvaro de Oliveira Ribeiro showered him with praise: 'He is an adult in a boy's body.' He explained that the deal had been long and complex but that the end result was something that had never been done before in Brazilian football.

Neto commented: '[Brazilian] football has always sold its "raw materials" as soon as there was a chance to make money. What Santos has done goes against the grain of national culture. It was an example for other clubs.'

The contract was signed; now there was just the project to get under way. There were two limbs to it: the player and the sponsors. The club from Baixada Santista set up a task force to look after its investment. Roles were assigned: there was someone to look after his appointments and diary, someone to accompany him to away matches and matches with the national side. The eyes of Santos would never let Neymar out of their sight. Then there was the work around developing Neymar, plus the media training so that he knew how to behave in front of the cameras and the microphones. He was to have elocution lessons with Cida Coelho so that he could pronounce words properly, along with English lessons so that he could get by.

Then there was the hardest aspect of all of the project: selling the Neymar brand. Neto commented: 'It was not difficult for Neymar because he is naturally charismatic. Something which you cannot buy at the supermarket. He is a natural media icon. How can we sell him? Analysing the body and soul, we can offer different qualities to different investors. Body: his hair, his extravagance, his tattoos, his constant use of social media: Instagram, Facebook, Twitter. Neymar is a child of his time, connected with technology, music and fashion. Soul: he is a synonym for bravery, happiness and speed.

'I remember when I spoke about the possible sponsorship by Red Bull. They said to me, "Neto, we only sponsor teams, not individuals. The only individual player we sponsored was Edgar Davids because of his predatory look. Neymar does not have that sort of image. We are a better fit for extreme sports athletes." OK, I switched on my iPad and looked up Santos–Guarani in the 2010 Brazil Cup on Youtube. Neymar scored five goals. I showed them one at a time. In the end the Red Bull manager said, "This is not a football player, this is an extreme sports athlete."

'Red Bull was the third personal sponsor after Nike and

Panasonic. The others followed after that. In 2011, every five or ten days or so, there was someone who wanted a piece of the action, who wanted to sponsor Neymar. It was not long before there were thirteen sponsors.'

And yet, despite the Neymar project having worked so well, in June 2013 Neymar packed his bags for Barcelona.

Neto explained, 'Santos showed Brazil and Brazilian football that it was possible for one of the best players in the world to stay in Brazil for a while. It was an important lesson to a system which is used to selling off players. There is no doubt that Santos profited from it. Much more than if they had sold Neymar in 2010. Santos were rewarded both on and off the pitch. They won six titles; membership grew from 20,000 to 66,000; their turnover grew from 70 million reais in 2009 to 198 million in 2012. The Santos brand sky-rocketed and TV rights, sales from licensed products and earnings from shirt sponsorship all increased: from 6 million to 40 million reais. The club is in the top 50 clubs in the world according to the latest research. It is not all Neymar's doing but his presence has certainly helped raise the profile of the club.'

Why let him go then?

'Because when a player has made up their mind, there is little you can do,' comes the reply. 'All you can do is wish them well and that's it. In addition, while our club can bear the costs of a player like Neymar, the market, the footballing environment and the structure of our football cannot. We need a more professional league and club to be able to compete with the Spanish *Liga* or the English Premier League, but this is Brazil and today this is not the case. We can't even compete with Ukraine teams. It's a shame.'

Chapter 18
Monster

'I am deeply disappointed today. I have spent my entire life in football but I have hardly ever seen someone as rude (from a sporting perspective) as this boy, Neymar. I have always worked with young players and I have never seen anything like it. What he did was unacceptable. Even the Santos players did not agree with his behaviour. It is time someone educated him or we will create a monster. It is true we are creating a monster in Brazilian football in the name of *futebol arte*. I believe in the art but not this. He is all-powerful both on and off the pitch. You journalists, the referees, the club, all of us need to educate him for the good of football because at the moment he is not a man, nor a great player: he is a product of all of this. What I saw today was bad, very bad.'

So spoke René Simões, coach for Atlético Goianiense, being controversial on local TV and radio and in front of the press microphones at Vila Belmiro on the evening of 15 September 2010. What could have happened that was so bad to cause Simões to repeat the word 'monster' at least five times in two minutes while referring to Neymar Jr? What had he done that was so bad? Let's start at the beginning.

It was the 22nd round of matches in the *Brasilerão* and Santos were playing Atlético Goianiense, a Goiânia team, from the state of Goiás, at Vila Belmiro. It should have been an easy match for Peixe, who incidentally had not won any of their last three matches.

But things got complicated. Peixe were two goals down at half-time. Neymar decided to take things into his own hands and got on with turning the tables. A few minutes into the second half and the score was 3–2 to Santos. Then Neymar was fouled on the edge of the area. He gestured clearly that he was going to take the free-kick, and placed the ball, but Marcel ran up and took the kick.

With five minutes to go to the end of the match, the same thing happened again. This time the Santos number 11 was in the box. Penalty. Neymar picked up the ball and walked to the spot. Change of plan: Léo, the number 3, ran over to Neymar and told him that the coach had decided that Marcel should take the kick.

This was where the problems started. Neymar dropped the ball on the floor and started shrugging his shoulders and waving his arms about and walked over to the bench. He gave the coach, Dorival Junior, a piece of his mind – better not to repeat his exact words.

Léo went over to Neymar, hugged him and tried to calm him down. Even Marquinos, who was on the touchline, tried to placate him but Neymar slipped past him and went to the centre of the pitch with a bottle of water in his hand. He had a go at Roberto Brun and Edu Dracena, the team captain, who tried to calm him down. Marcel converted the penalty and it was 4–2 to Santos. Neymar did not care; he continued to behave like a spoilt child having a strop.

After the penalty, he went into ball-hogging mode. He was on a one-man mission. The team did not exist anymore. The coach, from the sidelines, was at his wits' end and kept shouting instructions, but to no avail. The Santos fans were on the coach's side. They chanted the manager's name rather than that of their idol, Neymar. Outside the stadium, the fans chanted, 'Santos is more important than Neymar.'

At the end of the match, the number 11 ran straight off the pitch and into the changing rooms. He dismissed the waiting journalists without saying a word. A downbeat Dorival acted as spokesperson: 'It is a difficult, serious and grave situation which I would prefer to resolve internally with Neymar, his father and the club management. I do not feel comfortable talking about it. I know René has said something about what has happened. I think I would have done the same in his shoes.'

The journalists wanted blood, they wanted to know what was happening with Neymar.

'I don't know. I am doing everything I can to help him but once the situation is taken out of my hands, it will be difficult. Thank God that in all the seventeen years of my career, I have not had a problem with discipline. With Neymar, it's different. It is a new situation. We are all learning something new, including Neymar,' said Dorival.

Dorival explained why he let Marcel take the penalty: Neymar had had three misses out of six attempts, and even in training he was not getting a good percentage of conversions.

Neymar's rebellion did not go down well with his teammates either. Marcel was succinct and to the point: 'A player must accept the decisions of his coach. The hierarchy on a football field must be honoured, just like in a company.'

The next day, Neymar, the monster, was the topic of all the TV chat shows, the critics' newspaper columns and the fans' reactions. The newspapers trotted out the previous 'bad' behaviour of the number 11: the controversial lob of Corinthians defender Chicão, the lob of Avai defender Marcinho Guerreiro, etc. – provocations which set off the other team's players.

Antonio Lopes, the coach for the *Catarinense* team, accused Neymar of effectively saying, 'I am a millionaire and I can do what I want.'

The latest entry on this rap sheet had come on the Sunday prior to the Atlético Goianiense match: Neymar argued with João Marcos of Ceará and nasty words were exchanged. If it were not for their teammates, punches would have been thrown.

The Brazilian press had a field day: 'It is becoming a habit for Neymar to leave the pitch at the centre of some controversy or other.'

They called him a rebel, they said he had got too big for his boots. They said he had no respect for anyone anymore. Basically he was a proper 'bad boy'. Even his sponsors started to take a step back. Three companies that were going to sign with Neymar called the club's marketing team and said that he had gone mad and that they were no longer interested. Bad news followed bad news.

An insider leaked the exchanges with the captain and then with Dorival's assistant in the changing rooms at Vila Belmiro. Neymar, who had not showed up to the press meeting the previous evening, tweeted to calm the waters: 'The argument I had on the pitch is from someone who wants to win … it is for the good of the group as a whole … Dorival Junior is a person whom I admire and respect a great deal. He has my complete backing. Everything is fine. Thank God we are back to our winning ways. Let's carry on, *profe.*'

It was not enough for the commentators or the fans. Some of the fans even put up an offensive banner in front of the 'monster's' house.

Neymar was asked to apologise in front of the group and the public and the next day he obliged: 'I apologise to Dorival, Edu and my teammates and to the chairman and fans of Santos. I apologise to all those who love Neymar and the kids who look up to me. I ask for forgiveness because what happened last night was not the Neymar people want to see. Neymar is happiness, football with a smile across his face.'

This was the show for the journalists. In private, Neymar prayed to God for forgiveness.

Years later he still remembers that day, 15 September 2010. It was one of the worst days of his life. He remembers that, after the match, he got home and found his father and mother crying. Nadine, who had watched the match from the stands, told him, 'I did not recognise you on that pitch. That was not my son today. That was not the Juninho I brought up.' Her words cut through Neymar, much more than the torrent of abuse which ensued over the following days. Neymar recalls those horrible, interminable nights when he cried like he'd never cried before. The Santos chairman confirmed this: 'I found him the next day at eight in the morning. He was red-eyed and with a puffed face. He was sincerely sorry for what he had done.

'I explained to him that he would get much more out of the sport and be more successful if his image was one of happiness both on and off the pitch. Being a "bad boy" does not pay in the long run.'

Neymar thanked him. He said that if it had not been for his family, his supporters and the club, he might have thrown the towel in that day.

He made up with Dorival Junior, allegedly, right after the match when the coach called him into his office. Dorival decided to punish Neymar and use the incident to set an example. An act of this nature, whether it be from a kid in the youth teams or from Neymar, could not be tolerated. The coach had to have a firm hand. He decided to fine Neymar 50,000 reais and suspend him from the team.

Dorival explained, 'I believe it is in his [Neymar's]

interests, albeit not for the club, that we work without such an important player as Neymar. It is with a heavy heart that I punish him but I hope that this can help the boy grow.' Dorival added that his decision was fully supported by the club and that he had full authority.

On Sunday 19 September, Santos played Guarani at the Brinco de Ouro in Campinas. Neymar was not playing, having been suspended. He watched on as a fan and saw his team achieve a dull 0–0.

What now? Would Neymar play against Corinthians at Vila Belmiro, an important match in the *Brasilerão*? After training the day before the match, the press conference was held. The first question to the coach was 'Will Neymar play?'

Dorival was succinct and decisive: 'No, Neymar will not play.'

This reply marked the end of the honeymoon period between Santos and Dorival Junior. Luis Álvaro de Oliveira Ribeiro, the chairman, on hearing the news, went ballistic. He had agreed with the coach that Neymar would only be banned for one match. At least, that is the version of events he gives. He picked up the phone and called the vice-chairman and the board's coordinator to discuss the situation. The decision was taken: Dorival was out. He was called to the CT Rei Pelé that evening and at one in the morning the news was given that Dorival had been sacked.

'*Perdeu Dorival*' ('Dorival loses'); '*Neymar riu por último*' (Neymar has last laugh); '*Neymar derrumba Dorival*' ('Neymar overthrows Dorival'); '*Neymar "vence" queda de braço: Dorival fora!*' ('Neymar "wins" arm wrestle: Dorival out!') were the newspaper headlines.

As is the norm in these cases, club officials talked of a reciprocal decision in light of a relationship which was no longer working. Everyone else believed that Dorival lost the arm wrestle over Neymar. The club had to decide between a coach who had won two titles and an eighteen-year-old kid worth 80 million reais. The decision was easy. Better to have an icon, the fans' favourite, the prodigal player.

What were the consequences of this? In the São Paulo *Folha*, 'PVC', Paulo Vinicius Coelho, summed up in his column as follows: 'Neymar is now the king of the castle at Vila Belmiro, which is exactly what an eighteen-year-old kid should not be allowed to think.'

Chapter 19
Beatlemania

A conversation with Dorival Silvestre Junior

In the press conference after 'the event', the journalists asked Dorival if Neymar was a spoilt kid. Dorival replied straightaway with 'no'. They asked him if Neymar was rude. Again the same answer. They asked him if Neymar was unmanageable and Dorival replied that Neymar was a good kid who was sometimes a bit impulsive, like the football he played. He added, 'This is why we cannot accept certain behaviour, but we need to understand it.'

What was there to understand about Neymar's behaviour which caused such a stir and put his future in doubt?

Dorival Silvestre Junior, with his black and white hair and calm manner, is the manager for Fluminense now. He has just come in to the Bourbon Residence in Rio de Janeiro from afternoon training. A quick shower and change of clothes, two phone calls and then we get chance to talk about the insults during the Santos–Atlético Goianiense match.

Dorival begins: 'What do we need to understand? There was an eighteen-year-old kid who was trying to deal with immense pressure.

'When I arrived at Santos in December 2009 with the backing of Luis Álvaro de Oliveira Ribeiro, to replace Vanderlei Luxemburgo, Neymar was not that well known. He had just started in the first team about six months earlier.

In January I met him by chance in a shopping centre while he was shopping with his girlfriend, just like lots of kids his age. He was just wandering around without anyone bothering him or asking for his autograph or for a photo.

'By April of the same year, he finished training on pitch 1 and on pitch 2 there was a helicopter waiting to take him to Rio or São Paulo for a publicity event or TV show. In three months, his life had changed completely.'

What had happened?
'Santos had started to play well and entertain the crowd and win matches eight, nine, even ten nil. Neymar became the fans' idol. Wherever he went, at whatever hour, people would appear from nowhere to see him. At the airport, at the stadium, at training, in the hotel lobby when we played away matches. With all the young girls screaming at him, it was like Beatlemania all over again. It was difficult for him. And that was not all.

'After winning the Paulistão, the pressure got even worse. All of the TV programmes, all the papers and all the magazines talked about him. Everyone wanted him to be a guest on their programmes, all of them wanted him to be a sponsor for their product.

'Amidst all this, Chelsea came along and made him a mega offer: Europe, €35 million. Then the new dream contract with Santos.

'There were too many things going on at once. It was changing his world and it was changing him. In those last two months, the insidious appeal of everything which is dangerous about football: parties, girls, all sorts of things.'

So what did you do?
'I got his attention. I spoke to him and said that he

needed to focus on football, on training and his work ethic because the demands he had to face on the pitch would get harder and harder as each game passed. I told him that at the end of the day, that was his job and that thanks to his job, doors were opening. He could not let it drop.'

But it would appear that the lecture did not have the desired effect considering the pantomime on the pitch in the match against Atlético Goianiense?

'I was forced to intervene because he was having a go at Roberto Brun and Edu Dracena, the captain. He wanted to take the penalty at all costs. Before the match, we had agreed that the penalty taker was not Neymar. In the changing rooms afterwards, Neymar apologised for the insults; it was a moment of nervous tension, he said. My decision had already been taken.'

A decision which cost you your job?

'When you manage a group, you have to act appropriately with everyone concerned. You have to be consistent in your judgement. You cannot favour one over another. Neymar was a very important player for Santos but I had to punish him. He expected it and agreed. The entire club management expected the punishment. They had not appreciated his behaviour. The problems with the club management came later. It was a clear disciplinary sanction and not a technical sanction. We agreed two matches and not one but things went differently. And when I told the press that he would not be playing against Corinthians, who at that time were fighting for the title, the whole world caved in. The press were all over me as soon as I'd said it. "You cannot exclude the local idol."'

Do you regret your decision?

'No. I do not regret it. Obviously I would have liked to have finished my contract with Santos: we were playing an excellent championship up to that point. It was a job which I had just started and there was still a lot to do. I would have liked to have continued. But I cannot forget that my role is primarily that of an educator, especially with the young players. Such behaviour has to be marked and corrected. Even though what he did was not particularly serious and was within the bounds of normality, it was the result of what was happening to him at that time. He had become famous, rich, powerful and loved so quickly.'

After the 'event' he became a bad boy, an out-of-control rebel ...

'Here in Brazil, we have the attitude (and I believe it is not just us) to want too much from a personality. We take a person to the highest heights and then dash them down to the depths of hell just because they stepped out of line. There is no halfway house, no in between. This was exactly what happened to Neymar: from hero to zero in but a few hours. Even the TV psychologists explained his behaviour ...'

How do you judge that event after all this time?

'I believe it was very important for Neymar and me. Neymar matured thanks to the reaction of his family and his friends; he understood the seriousness of what he had done and what was happening to him. He grew up a lot, he grew as a player and as a person. He went back to his roots, to normality. It was a decisive moment in his career. A jump forward.

'The positive outcome can be seen by how he plays in the national team today, where he can make the difference, and also at Barcelona where he is getting used to a different environment with great ease.'

Chapter 20
Doha

Brazil–Argentina: Messi vs. Neymar Jr. For the first time they were face to face. In Doha, Qatar, at the Khalifa International Stadium.

Truth be told, the duel people had been waiting for was that between the current number 10s, Messi and Ronaldinho – the former Barcelona teammates. Neymar was still a novice who needed more experience. His name was not splashed all over the stadium posters: it was only his second match for the Brazilian national team.

His debut for the senior side was on 10 August 2010. Brazil against the USA in New Meadowlands, New Jersey. After the debacle in South Africa, Dunga resigned and the Brazilian Football Confederation decided to appoint Mano Menezes. The new man came from Corinthians, where he had won three titles in three years (first the *Campeonato Brasileiro Série B* and then, following the promotion of the team to the top division, the Paulistão and Brazil Cup in 2009). Things were looking good for Brazil, especially with the 2014 World Cup, on home soil, coming up.

Against the USA, the line-up contained the names everyone was expecting to see: Neymar and Paulo Henrique – the players Dunga had decided not to take to the South Africa World Cup. One was playing in the number 11 shirt, the same as he did for Santos, the other in the number 10.

At the end of the match, the two friends were as happy as

Larry. Ganso commented, 'I did not expect my first match to be as good as this but Mano gave us complete freedom; he told us to play as we knew how to. We were able to show off our *futebol alegre* ['joyful football'] which we have been playing throughout the year with Santos.

'Wearing the number 10 for Brazil is a huge responsibility but, thank God, we managed to play a good match and show my talent.'

And Neymar? The boy wonder did not expect to score on his debut, and certainly not with his head, but that is what happened. In the 28th minute, Robinho passed to André Santos, who was pushing forward on the left. He crossed into the box and Neymar beat the defender to the ball and headed past the US goalkeeper Tim Howard. The number 11 fell to his knees and raised his arms to the sky, and then kissed the Brazilian crest on his shirt before being mobbed by his teammates, Ganso and Alexander Pato. Pato added a second for Brazil in the 47th minute to give a final score of 2–0.

Neymar commented, 'My goal was to make sure we could relax. Everything went well after that.' Neymar's pre-match nerves were well gone. He added, 'It will be a lot easier now.'

It was easy indeed for Mano Menezes, who after the match received a standing ovation. The press effused praise for the return of *futebol alegre*: speed, dribbling, *pedaladas* (stepovers) … after the defensive Brazil of Dunga, the poetry and attacking football were back.

The following matches were not so easy for Neymar. In the friendlies against Iran and Ukraine, he was not selected. This was not due to his performance against the USA but because of the controversy surrounding the Dorival Junior affair. Another punishment to enable the boy to grow and sort himself out.

He made his return to the team in Doha on 17 November 2010 in a match against Argentina.

Before the match, emotions were high, especially as Ronaldhino was making his return to the national team after several months. Microphone in hand, Brazil shirt on, Neymar could hardly get a word out: he was choked with emotion as he stood next to his idol: 'I am one of his fans. I love his football, his career, him as a person, everything he has done for the Brazilian team. I remember his dribbling, his lobs, the goal he scored against England in the South Korea World Cup.'

He shook hands with 'Ronnie' and passed him the microphone. The Milan player confessed in a low voice, 'I have followed his career from the beginning, as well as the new generation of players at Santos. It is pure *futebol alegre*, it is football art.

'I feel privileged to be able to play again for Brazil and to be part of this group. We hope to be able to bring great joy to the Brazilian people.'

At the Khalifa International Stadium, Leo Messi was the one bringing happiness. 'La Pulga' finally got to beat his eternal rivals at the fifth time of asking. The previous contests had seen Argentina lose three and draw one. Even at the Beijing Olympics in 2008, when Argentina *had* beaten Brazil (on the way to the gold medal), Messi had not managed to score in the match.

This time he managed to. In second-half stoppage time, Douglas in midfield made a mistake. Argentina gained possession and went on the counterattack. Messi stormed up the field. He covered half the pitch and left Lucas behind. He weaved around David Luiz and Thiago Silva and then slotted it in past Victor, the Brazilian goalkeeper, who could do nothing but watch it go in.

Messi had won the duel with his former Barça teammate, who was substituted in the second half. Ronaldinho's performance was admirable – perfect long passes, free kicks and an attempt on goal with his heel – but it was not to be.

Neymar, on the other hand, was not on the same form as in his first match. He was not key to the match; indeed he was almost playing a secondary role. On the left wing, he was the Brazilian player highest up the pitch. But he did not penetrate. He fell down too often and was substituted before the end. A leading commentator, Juca Kfouri, said Neymar was in need of more experience and maturity.

At the end of the day, Neymar had only been involved with the Brazil set-up for two years.

In 2008, Lucho Nizzo was putting together a team of players to take part in the Under-17 World Cup in Nigeria the following year. Neymar had made a good impression playing for Santos in 'La Copinha', so it was only right that the coach of the youth teams should try him out in the under-16s.

The first commitment was the Mediterranean International Cup, a youth tournament played in Spain, on the Costa Brava, since 2001. It is one of the most prestigious football exhibition tournaments in the world, where many young kids have showcased their talents on their way to becoming professionals: the likes of Cesc Fàbregas, Gerard Piqué, Juan Mata, Marcelo, Jordi Alba and Lucas Leiva.

In 2003, a certain Leo Messi turned up. Nizzo remembers it well because that was the first year the Brazilians took part in the tournament. Josep Colomer, manager of the youth teams at Barcelona, spoke well of him. The fifteen-year-old amazed the crowds with his skills and goals. Five years later, it was Neymar and Philippe Coutinho who were to set sparks flying.

In the 2008 edition, 144 teams (split into various

categories: *alevin, infantil, cadete* and *juvenil*) from nineteen countries took part in the tournament. On 19 March, the opening ceremony took place at Palamós: the teams paraded around the pitch, huge papier mâché mascots, fireworks, *sardanas* (a Catalonian dance), cheerleaders from Barcelona and, to finish, a match between *los juveniles* from the local team and Brazil. Finishing 1–0 to Brazil, it was a taster of what was to come.

Philippe Coutinho and Neymar, number 8 and number 10 respectively, were the main players for Brazil. Strangers until Nizzo selected them for the squad, they hit it off immediately, both on and off the pitch. Coutinho, a kid from Rio de Janeiro who played in the Vasco da Gama youth team (and now plays for Liverpool following stints at Inter and Espanyol), was the midfield playmaker, while Neymar, according to the coach at the time, was 'a hanging attacker, who cuts upfield in search of goal every time he gets the ball'.

Within a few days of meeting each other, they got on like a house on fire. The one-twos, the exchanges between them, were a constant feature of the matches. How many passes, tricks, etc. did they make over the course of the tournament? When Neymar was asked, he simply laughed.

Brazil got through the qualifiers without any hiccups and got to the semi-finals in Calonge. On the day of the match, a huge storm turned the pitch into a quagmire. The ball got stuck and bogged down; it was almost impossible to get the ball out of the puddles and control it with any technique or Brazilian flair. The opponents, Konoplet, a Russian team, were a physically stronger team and took control of the game. They scored first. In the second half, the weather improved slightly. Darkness fell and it started to get cold. Turning the game around was not going to be easy. Coutinho managed to strike the ball and the Russian goalkeeper could not keep it out. One-all. Neymar got injured a few minutes later and left the pitch.

It went down to penalties. Luis Guillerme, the goalkeeper for Brazil, managed to hold on to one of the Russians' strikes. The players in the green and gold went wild. They were in the final. But with Neymar having had to be carried off the pitch, his participation looked doubtful.

The sun was shining at the Palamós Municipal Stadium on Sunday 23 March 2008. The final was to take place later that day: Brazil versus Lokomotiv Moscow. Neymar was fit.

The match was not easy but the two *wunderkinder* knew what to do. Coutinho played a ball through to Neymar, who was brought down just outside the area. Number 11 for Brazil, Wellington Alves da Silva (at the time with Fluminense, now with Real Murcia on loan from Arsenal) lined up the free kick. The Lokomotiv goalkeeper did not get anywhere near. He had held the fort up to this point but there was nothing he could do this time.

It was the winning goal. Brazil celebrated. Neymar celebrated. Pictures show him with fuzzy hair and a smile plastered across his face, his gold medal around his neck. Next to him are Coutinho, flying the *Ordem e Progreso* flag, and the manager, along with the cup. Neymar thanked God that it had all gone according to plan; but who knew what the future would hold.

The future for Brazil was the 2009 Under-17 World Cup in Nigeria. On 24 October 2009, in the Teslim Balogun Stadium in Lagos, Brazil's opening match was against Japan. Neymar, wearing number 11, put his team ahead in the 67th minute. The goal featured all of the three stars who had shone in the Costa Brava tournament: Neymar, Coutinho and Wellington. Nizzo wanted these three in his team come what may.

Wellington picked up the ball in defence and then passed to Coutinho in midfield. He turned, moved forward and launched the ball to his friend, Neymar, who was waiting. Neymar ran to the ball and in front of Japan's goal he did something incredible. He flicked the ball with the end of his right foot past the goalkeeper and then shimmied the other way and slotted the ball in the net. It was almost a carbon-copy of Pelé's near miss against Ladislao Mazurkiewicz's Poland in the 1970 World Cup. Neymar's goal, though, went in.

However, it was his only goal of the tournament. After a 3–2 win against Japan, Brazil lost two matches: to Mexico and Switzerland. Brazil finished third in Group B and headed home.

Ten months later, Neymar played his first match for the Brazil first team.

In time, there would be successes to make up for the dis-appointment of the Under-17 World Cup. Not least in 2011.

Chapter 21

2011

There are very few occasions in life where you get the chance to experience so many emotions, so much joy, so much happiness, in only twelve months. It is rare to receive, in such a short time frame, so many important life lessons which you will carry with you for the rest of your life – for better or for worse.

It is even rarer when you are only nineteen.

In 2011, Neymar was lucky enough to experience this. This was a year in which everything happened for Neymar. He became a father, won four historic titles, entered international football, achieved millionaire contracts, became a footballing icon on a par with a popstar and was party to a debacle which sent shock waves through Brazilian football. All of this at the speed of light: a whirlwind of events which increased exponentially compared to what had happened the year before.

Let's start at the beginning.

17 January 2011, Jorge Basadre Stadium, Tacna

To get the year off to a good start, Neymar Jr scored all four of Brazil's goals against Paraguay in the first match of the Under-20 South American Championship. The Buenos Aires sports daily *Olé* went with the headline 'Neymaradona'. Ney Franco, the technical coach, had called up both Neymar and Philippe Coutinho for the tournament. Coutinho was ruled out, however, due to injury. Franco also chose the cream of Brazil's young players: Lucas Moura, Fernando, Oscar and Casemiro.

The tournament would be the ticket to the 2012 London Olympics. It looked good for Neymar at the start as he predicted 'I have to play my football' – and kept the promise right from the outset.

First he scored a penalty after a foul on Casemiro (now playing for Real Madrid), and celebrated with his *la dança do créu'* ('Mc Créu's dance') with music from Mc Créu. Then, in the 33rd minute, Lucas put the ball in the area, Neymar showed some nifty footwork and made it 2–0. The third came via a header. The fourth was a beauty: Rafael Galhardo on the left delivered a killer pass, Neymar cut into the box and, as the keeper came out, he lobbed it over him.

Brazil 4 Paraguay 2 was the final score. Next it was Colombia. Again Brazil took the points, winning 3–1, with Neymar wrapping things up with the last goal.

A draw against Bolivia and victory against Ecuador meant that Brazil finished top of their group. Six teams went through to the final heats. Brazil's next match was against Chile: it finished 5–1 to Brazil, with Neymar getting two. He was now up to seven for the tournament. His eighth and ninth were to come at Arequipa in the south of Peru – the birthplace of Mario Vargas Llosa. Everyone in this city knew the author who, in 2010, won the Nobel Prize.

Everyone wanted to see the new Pelé, Neymar, who arrived in Peru relatively unknown but instantly became a massive star. Seeing how much interest the match and Neymar had whipped up, the *Comembol* decided to change the time of the match with Brazil, switching it to prime time.

On 12 February 2011, Brazil played Uruguay. Uruguay had a one-point advantage over Brazil when they got to the last match of the tournament, as Brazil had lost to Argentina. Uruguay were the favourites to qualify in first position and earn a place at the Olympics. It was not to be: Uruguay got trounced 6–0. Three goals from Lucas Moura, one from Danilo and two from Neymar. Brazil won the tournament for the third time in succession, their eleventh title since the inaugural competition in 1954, and thus earned their place in the 2012 Olympic Games. Neymar was the leading goalscorer with nine goals and was voted the best player in the tournament.

Ney Franco confessed in an interview with *El País*, 'At the beginning some people thought Neymar was the rebellious type with his casual style, styled hair and relaxed attitude. In reality, he is someone who has a huge personality and he really showed it in that tournament. He was the centre of attention, he was a great footballer, but he was able to play for the team and be part of the group.'

The Brazilian critics stated, 'At just nineteen, Neymar is already used to stunning the crowds and creating a show with the team. He demolished Uruguay's defence, he was crucial in the Paraguay, Colombia and Chile matches. He leaves the tournament with an extremely promising career ahead of him, more than anyone could have expected.'

So much praise, and yet Neymar, while celebrating with his medal and the Brazilian flag in hand, commented, 'There are no stars here. We have created a fantastic family in two months and this is the result of work which started on 13 December [the day the pre-tournament training camp started]. Now our dream is to play at the Olympics and bring home the gold medal.'

24 February 2011, Forte dos Andradas, Guarujá

'Even without doing military service, Neymar's talent and skills can do a lot for our country. He can help promote our country in the world more than it already has been.'

These were the words of General Santos in front of the TV cameras during Neymar's visit to Forte dos Andradas.

Neymar turned up to the 1st Brigade of the anti-aircraft artillery camp sporting sunglasses, T-shirt and white shoes, the famous Mohican, now with little dreadlocks, a huge watch and a gold necklace. The cadets patted him on the shoulder, shook his hand, gave him a hug, asked for an autograph or a photo and offered him a brigade shirt and beret. Neymar was visiting the fort to get his compulsory military service exemption. While he was there he was treated to a film of Pelé, who, unlike Neymar, did do military service. (In 1959 at Fort Itaipu in Praia Grande, Pelé was there and ended up playing football for the military.)

Eventually Neymar obtained the signed document exempting him from the marching, training and the dorms … all with the kind blessing of the commander of the fort. The commander admitted that football could achieve more than arms – in the case of Neymar, anyway.

27 March 2011, Emirates Stadium, London

It was his third match with the national team and, fittingly, the Brazilian football prodigy scored three goals. The match was against Scotland, the venue Arsenal's Emirates Stadium, London. Neymar took part in his favourite pastime: scoring goals. With great ease he racked them up. The first came from a ball from André Santos on the left, which he brought down and then launched a missile into the far corner of the goal. The second was a one-man show. He danced and skipped with the ball into Scotland's area and the defender,

Adam, brought him crashing to the floor. Neymar wasted no time in converting the penalty.

The TV commentators were stunned by the technique and deadly effectiveness of Neymar's play and, while the match was under way, started to talk about his future: they concluded that his future was in the UK.

Interestingly, a large number of the fans from London booed Neymar for the entire match. At one point, while dribbling in the area, Neymar was hit by a banana: a pure act of racism. Neymar commented, 'It is always sad when these sorts of things happen. I cannot come here and see these sorts of things.' The Scottish fans denied any act of racism. They said they had had enough of Neymar's constant diving, simulating fouls – that old chestnut. But perhaps what irritated the Scots most of all was the elaborate dribbling and his style of play which destroys opponents.

15 May 2011, Vila Belmiro, Santos

'Santos ... Santos ... Goal!
Now:
Who gives the ball, it's Santos
Santos is the new champion
Glorious Alvinegro Praiano
Absolute champion this year'

As Santos's anthem, 'Leão do mar', says, the glorious Alvinegro Praiano are champions this year. The popular tune was composed by José Maugeri Neto and Maugeri Sobrinho in 1955. Now, in 2011, the music boomed around Vila Belmiro stadium. Edu Dracena, the captain, on a stage in the centre of the pitch, lifted the Paulista Cup for the second year running. It is the nineteenth trophy and the sixth 'double' (back-to-back titles) in Santos's history.

The deciding goal was scored in the second leg against Corinthians (after the first leg had finished 0–0) and it was Neymar who scored it.

Santos were 1–0 up following a 43rd-minute goal from Arouca. Neymar had already missed a chance to make it two: alone in the box, he tried to put the ball between the legs of Julio Cesar, the goalkeeper, but Cesar sensed what Neymar was doing and deflected it for a corner.

Now, in the 83rd minute, Cesar was not so lucky: Neymar struck the ball with his right foot and, although it was not the strongest of shots, it slipped through Cesar's hands and then trickled over the line despite Cesar's desperate dive to try and claw the ball back.

In the 86th minute, Morais clawed one back for Corinthians but it was too late to try for the draw. A triumphant Neymar was hoisted on the shoulders of his teammates and hugs and kisses of joy flew.

It had not been an easy Paulistão. After the dismissal of Dorival Junior, a succession of managers had failed to settle into the role: three in total. Marcelo Martelotte, Adilson Batista, then Martelotte again before Muricy Ramalho took the role on 10 April 2011. The team had been transformed: Robinho, who was one of the stars in 2010, went back to Europe; André, another friend of Neymar's, was sold to Dynamo Kiev right after Santos's 2010 Brazil Cup success; Elano was bought from Galatasary to bolster the midfield (he was no foreigner to Santos having played from 2001 to 2005) – this was a good buy but the dream pairing between Elano and Paulo Henrique was not to be as Henrique tore ligaments in his knee in a match against Gremio on 25 August 2010, meaning he could not play for another seven months. He would return in March 2011.

Neymar was engaged with the Brazil Under-20s and could

not play the first six league matches. Muricy Ramalho was unable to field his strongest line-up until the quarter-finals of the Paulistão, where Santos beat Ponte Preta with a goal from Neymar. Then it was on to São Paulo: Elano and Ganso sorted things out. The final awaited and Santos did not miss their opportunity to get another 'double', played out to the unmistakable *zumpa pà-pà – zumpa pà-pà* anthem.

22 June 2011, Pacaembu, São Paulo

Forty-eight years after Caetano's own goal and Pelé's double against the Uruguayan team Peñarol, Santos won the Libertadores against the same team.

It was 15 June at the Centenario Stadium in Montevideo and the stadium was a sea of black and yellow, the colours of the home team. When the two teams jogged onto the pitch, the light from the fireworks and flares lit up the Montevideo night sky. The roaring welcome sent shivers down the Santos players' spines. The Santos boys did not let it get to them. It was 0–0 at the final whistle. It could have been better but for Peixe it was a good result as the second leg was in Pacaembu.

For the second leg, the stadium was teeming. Santos were in a creative mood and made many chances but at first nothing came off. Shortly after half-time, though, Neymar managed to open up the game by scoring the first goal: Arouca carved out a lovely little manoeuvre from the midfield and found the number 11 free on the left; on the volley he smacked the ball past the goalkeeper into the right corner of the net. Goaaaaal!

The players were ecstatic and it was clear that the game was there for the taking. Danilo drove home the second and it looked as though it was all over. But there was still time for a comeback. In the 79th minute, while trying to clear his area, Santos defender Durval scored an own goal.

The fans could not believe it and some turned their backs on the pitch: they could not bear to watch. They only turned round when the Argentinian referee, Sergio Pezzotta, blew the final whistle.

Pure emotion took over: tears poured – and punches flew. A Santos fan invaded the pitch and attacked a player from Peñarol, who fought back. The gauntlet had been thrown down and the battle commenced. The police had to get involved to break up the two teams. It took a long time for peace and calm to be restored and the awards ceremony to take place.

Neymar knelt on the green carpet and raised his arms to the heavens. Muricy hugged Pelé and then accompanied him to the centre of the pitch. O Rei, with his red jacket on, waved to the crowds and when he was interviewed for TV channel Fox Deportes and asked about Neymar, he wore his heart on his sleeve: 'As everyone knows and as everyone can see, he is a great player with a huge talent. In the first half, he was not at his best because Peñarol defended very well. In the second half, he opened up the match and scored a brilliant goal. We will see if he can do the same when playing for Brazil. Let's hope he is not like Messi who plays brilliantly for Barcelona but not that well with Argentina.'

The journalist dared to ask the question everyone was thinking: 'Will he be better than you?' Pelé smiled and said, 'To do that he will need to score more than 1,283 goals.'

The Old King did not want to give up his crown quite yet.

A few days later Neymar was presented with his own crown. It was gold with an 'N' just like that of Napoleon. 'Reymar' was engraved on the crown and, to the side, the verdict of the São Paulo weekly magazine *Veja*, of 28 June: 'Finally we have a star who is of Pelé's calibre.'

17 July 2011, Estádio Ciudad de La Plata

It was a terrible afternoon: one of those days where the ball just did not want to go in the goal. It was cleared off the line, miraculously saved or chances were fluffed. In the ensuing shoot-out, four penalties were missed. Elano, Thiago Silva, André Santos and Fred could not do anything right. Brazil bombed out of the 2011 Copa America. It was the quarter-final and Brazil lost to Tata Martino's Paraguay, who went on to lose the final against Uruguay.

At the beginning of the tournament, which was held in Argentina, the most talked about names were Neymar and Paulo Henrique. Everyone was convinced that together they could change the outcome of a match and turn things around for Brazil. However, on Sunday 17 July, Brazil exited the Copa America without Neymar and Henrique having shown the brilliance that they regularly demonstrated for Santos – Neymar in particular.

Brazil just did not look themselves against Paraguay. In the 83rd minute Neymar was substituted for Fred. He watched the penalties from the bench, with Ganso, who came off in the first half of extra time. Mano Menezes had granted the number 11 plenty of licence to attack alongside Alexandre Pato. Neymar got his chance after only three minutes, but missed. He missed the second and third chances as well. In the second half, Pato set Neymar up beautifully but his shot was parried by Villar, the Paraguay goalkeeper.

Neymar paid dearly for his mistakes and things started to go wrong. His dribbling was not effective, he mistimed his runs and his passes went short or long into the hands of the opposition: he lost the ball nine times in total. When Brazil needed him, he was not there. Neymar's record at the end of the tournament was not great: two goals against Ecuador in the last Group B match and thirteen attempts on goal.

The critics were not amused: 'Too few goals for someone who is meant to lead the way for Brazil,' was their verdict.

27 July 2011, Vila Belmiro, Santos

A show? A spectacle? A memorable event? A historic match like in the films? An ode to football? However people chose to describe it, it was difficult to think of another match like Santos vs. Flamengo in the twelfth round of Brasilerão matches in 2011.

The 4–5 win for Flamengo reminded the older heads in the crowd of Santos's 7–6 win over Palmeiras in 1958. Two things were clear: Neymar played his best match for Santos, and Ronaldinho put in the type of performance he used to give when playing for Barcelona.

El Gaucho scored three goals, the first taking advantage of mistakes by Edu Dracena and the goalkeeper; the second from a free-kick which split the wall; and the third driven hard along the ground into the corner.

Neymar was on fire as well: from the ground, he switched the ball and set Borges up for a simple finish; he then earned a penalty, only to see Elano clip the bar with a Panenka-style kick; Neymar also scored two goals himself. The second, from a counterattack, put Santos 4–3 up with half an hour of the match left to play (prior to Ronaldinho's crucial second and third goals). Neymar's first was a work of art.

Neymar received the ball near the touchline, just inside the Flamengo half. He was marked closely by two players: Leo Moura and Williams. The players closed in on Neymar in a pincer movement. He needed to get out into the space; it looked impossible but somehow he managed it. He slipped between the two and ran forward. He saw Borges and played a one-two. Renato quickly closed in but Neymar skimmed round him and on to Ronaldo Angelim. A bit of dribbling and then the masterpiece: a flick to one side and Neymar passed around the other side of him. With a few metres to go, Neymar saw the defenders diving in and the goalkeeper coming off his line and lobbed it into the back of the net.

The goal earned Neymar the FIFA Ferenc Puskás Award for 2011.

On 9 January 2012, in the Congress building in Zurich, Neymar attended the yearly awards ceremony. Wearing a black jacket with white shirt and grey tie, and sporting styled hair with red highlights, he sat in one of the front rows. He was one of the star attractions as not only had he been nominated for the Puskás Award but he had also been shortlisted for the Ballon d'Or.

Ruud Gullit gave out the awards on the stage. The three finalists for the Puskás Award were Leo Messi, Wayne Rooney and Neymar. Messi earned his place with the goal he scored on 8 March in the Champions League against Arsenal – a fantastic flick and volley to beat the Gunners' keeper. The Red Devils' centre forward was in the running for his overhead kick in the derby against Manchester City on 12 February.

The videos of the three goals were shown and then Kate Murray, the journalist co-hosting with Gullit, introduced the person who would present the award: it was Hugo Sánchez, the greatest Mexican player of all time.

The former Real Madrid player commented, 'Scoring a beautiful goal makes you very happy but receiving this award is the best. I talk from experience.' The TV cameras zoomed in on Messi, Neymar and Rooney. 'The FIFA Puskás Award for 2011 goes to ... Neymar.'

The kid from Santos removed his earphones (worn for translation purposes) and shook Rooney's hand. He got up and passed by Gerard Piqué and Andres Iniesta. Doing his jacket up, he walked on to the stage. He said hello to Hugo Sánchez, Gullit and Murray, then looked out at the audience.

'I am very happy to be given this award. I was up against two of the greatest stars in football, of whom I am a great fan. I want to thank God and all those who are here. Have a great night.' So spoke an emotional Neymar. He took his award and headed off to party.

24 August 2011, Hospital São Luiz, São Paulo

'Nasceeeeuu !!! Davi Lucca …' was how Neymar announced the birth of his first son. He posted a photo online with him holding the baby, still wearing the hospital cap and gown.

The next photos were of his father and Paulo Henrique, friend and godfather to his child. Neymar published a note on his official site in Portuguese, English and Spanish stating that mother and son were doing well and that he would like to thank God 'for the little blessing in his life aka David Lucca; 2 kilos and 810 grams of pure joy and courage.'

Neymar was over the moon and he said as much in a tweet which topped the trending on the internet in Brazil after only a few hours. David Lucca was the most important thing in his life; but becoming a father at nineteen was not easy.

When Neymar heard that Carolina Dantas (then seventeen) was pregnant, he did not know what to think. He was scared. He was not ready for such responsibility, and Carolina was a casual partner. They had met through mutual friends when she was sixteen. He began sending her texts and eventually they started going out together, but it did not last long.

When Carolina discovered she was pregnant, she first thought of keeping it quiet and not telling Juninho, but then she realised that one day her son would want to know who his father was. She told him and he behaved like 'a true gentleman' (according to Carolina when she appeared on the TV program *Domingão do Faustão*).

Neymar still had to face his and Carolina's families. He first confronted his mother, Nadine, who burst into tears. With his father, it was not as easy, especially as his father had warned him to be careful and not make stupid mistakes which could have serious consequences.

A ticking off was inevitable and O Pai duly gave Neymar Jr what for, but then the emotion, the hugs and the paternal advice of a father who wanted the best for his son gushed forth. Neymar Pai told Juninho that whatever he decided to do (i.e. whether he married Carolina or not), the little boy would always be his grandson.

Neymar's fears faded and Neymar Pai accompanied Juninho to the Dantas family home. Neymar decided to acknowledge his son and to pay a monthly payment for his upkeep.

Neymar decided to go public, although without revealing the name of the mother. Neymar stayed close to Carolina throughout the pregnancy and at 11.00am on 24 August, Neymar was in the delivery room to welcome David Lucca to the world.

The young mother (now nineteen) and medical student commented, 'Juninho is a marvellous, caring, doting father and a friend who has stood by me. When he was at Santos, he would come and see him as often as he could, he was caring and showered him with gifts. Sometimes he stayed the night to sleep with David.'

Neymar had his son baptised at the *Igreja Batista Peniel* and when the baby was but a month old, on 7 September 2011, he took him to CT Rei Pelé so that he could meet his teammates.

On 4 March 2012, David Lucca was paraded when Santos

took the pitch at Vila Belmiro prior to the match against Corinthians. He brought the team luck and Santos won 1–0. David Lucca had become a sort of mascot for Santos, as Neymar Jr had once been for União Mogi.

28 September 2011, Mangueirão Stadium, Belém

The *Superclásico das Américas* is a trophy which dates back to 1913. It was founded by the Argentinian president, Julio Roca, to develop football in Argentina and in Brazil. The first tournament was held on 27 September 1914, a few days before the death of its founder. The match was held on the Gimnasia y Esgrima in Buenos Aires and Brazil won 1–0 with a goal from Rubens Salles.

With various formulas and different outcomes each year, the trophy pitted Brazil against Argentina right up until 1976. Then it stopped, just like that.

In 2011, though, it was rekindled thanks to an agreement between the Argentinian and Brazilian federations. The biggest challenge of them all was back on. The first match was to be held in the Mario Kempes Stadium in Córdoba on 14 September, with the return leg in Belem in Mangueirão on 28 September.

In Argentina, in front of 50,000 spectators, the match ended 0–0. The blue and whites put out a 'B' team without any of their Europe-based stars, while Brazil put out a fairly strong team, albeit with up-and-coming players: Lucas and Cortes had their debut. Iconic players like Ronaldinho were also there.

Neymar played in the return leg and scored the second goal in a 2–0 win. Cortes supplied Diegou with a cutting pass and Diegou drove the ball hard into the box, along the ground. Neymar slipped in between defender and goalkeeper to score.

Mano Menezes finally got the satisfaction of beating a top international team and Neymar got another trophy to add to his already full collection.

In 2012, Neymar would double his tally for the tournament before also finding the net in the penalty shoot-out that followed the second leg – his being the deciding kick of the *Superclásico*.

9 November 2011, Vila Belmiro

At 11.30am the deal was sealed with a handshake.

At 3.00pm the deal was officially announced.

Luis Álvaro de Oliveira Ribeiro, the Santos chairman, with his sleeves rolled up, kicked off the press conference: 'Whereas Neymar shows his talent on the pitch, destroying opposition defences, his family shows its loyalty and passion for Santos off the pitch.

'I would like to thank them from the bottom of my heart. I said that the happiest day of my life was 22 June in Pacaembu, when we won in the Libertadores after 48 years, but today is an even happier day for me because a dream has become reality.

'Neymar is staying with us until the 2014 World Cup. He has signed a contract and it is a done deal. He is not going to Real, nor Barcelona. He is with Santos.'

Ribeiro's Santos had fought back, in quixotic style, against the economic power of the European clubs. How? By paying more. Neymar's salary jumped from 1.5 million reais a month to 3 million a month; with the equivalent of €14.9 million a year, he was now the eighth best paid player in the world.

Peixe went to town on the advertising rights under the contract, granting Neymar 30 per cent. The break clause was bolstered as well. And the termination date of the contract was brought forward: before it was 2015, now it was August 2014.

It was a home run for Luis Álvaro de Oliveira Ribeiro, who, on 2 December, was standing for re-election as chairman. In the press room, Ribeiro, Neymar Jr and Neymar Pai sat patiently before the announcement. Neymar Jr was wearing a baseball cap on backwards and a black T-shirt and chewing gum. He calmly explained his feelings: 'I wanted to stay here. I had always said that. I thank the two Spanish clubs for their interest. It is an honour. But I never really thought about leaving to become the best in the world. Here I have my family, my son and my friends. I could not imagine leaving to become the best in the world. I just want to play in the best championships. Santos is doing that. We won the Libertadores and we are now playing the Club World Cup.'

Case closed … for the time being.

18 December 2011. International Stadium, Yokohama

'Today we learned how to play football. Barcelona was the better team. Its players are amazing. It is the best team in the world. This is the match which we learn from.'

The final of the FIFA Club World Cup 2011 had just finished. Neymar, with his Mohican hair flattened, plaster on his nose to help him breathe and a gloomy face, answered the TV journalists' questions from the sidelines. He admitted, grudgingly that Santos had just received a masterclass in how to play football. He then had to go and receive the runners-up trophy and the trophy for third best player of the tournament. He had to say hello to Leo Messi, who was the best player of the tournament beyond a shadow of a doubt and who would collect the Club World Cup trophy.

Neymar had to settle for runner-up this time as he

watched the Argentinian put in an amazing performance. 'La Pulga' was the complete forward, and he scored two of Barcelona's four goals against Santos. The first goal was a delightful lob over Rafael, Santos's goalkeeper, and the second was a quick rifle through the defence.

While Messi constantly received passes to his feet, Neymar did not even get one playable ball. Barcelona dominated the space and left Neymar isolated, a lost soul in a sea of green. Without the ball, it was a bit difficult to play football!

In the first half, the kid from Mogi das Cruzes' only moment was when he picked up the ball on the halfway line, but he was quickly blocked by Puyol and Piqué. In the second half, he got the only chance of the match for Santos, but he mistimed the shot against Victór Valdés coming forward. And that was that.

The only thing to add was the close-up shots of Neymar's face after every Barça goal.

The next day all the praise was for Pep Guardiola's team, who had just won their thirteenth title. *O Globo* in Rio de Janeiro laid it on thick: 'There is no other team quite like Barcelona in this world.' The *Clarín* in Buenos Aires went with 'Messi carries Barcelona to title'. *El País* preferred 'Barcelona's out-of-this-world football ends Santos's dream'.

That dream of repeating Pelé's achievement of winning the Club World Cup after 48 years (when Santos beat Milan in 1963) was shattered. The only consolation for Neymar was that Santos managed to get this far. He went home with the booby prize: Leo Messi's shirt …

Chapter 22
The gift of improvisation

A conversation with Muricy Ramalho

On entering, the security checks are strict. Before going past the double iron gates which surround the cream-coloured skyscrapers, you have to wait. There is time to take a quick glance at the road, where a group of kids are playing on a makeshift pitch on the edge of a *favela*. The rich and the poor right next to each other, one step from the ultra-modern, filiform Octávio Frias de Oliveira bridge, which stands elegantly over *rio Pinheiros* in São Paulo.

After checking on the phone, the security guard confirms, 'Mr Ramalho is in the Gourmet hall.'

The hall is accessed via the gardens. Muricy Ramalho comes and opens the door to an enormous room with settees and armchairs and an American kitchen. American coffee and glasses of water are served and the manager who has won four trophies in just over two years sits down on the other side of the table.

On 31 May 2013 Ramalho finished his adventure with Peixe. He thought he would take some time out to spend with his family, but things did not pan out like that. On 9 September, he accepted São Paulo Football Club's offer to go and manage them. But this is another story for another time. Let's talk about his arrival at Santos in April 2011, and about Neymar.

'Before I arrived at Santos, like everybody else who saw

him, I thought he was a good player. But when I watched him close up, I realised he was much more of a player than I could have imagined.

'Why? Because I saw him every day doing things that I had never seen being done before. I, myself, did not play much football [Muricy Ramalho played from 1973 to 1985 at São Paulo and then for Puebla in Mexico] but I have coached a lot and I have seen all sorts of footballers; but what Neymar did I had never seen before.'

What was it that impressed you about him?
'It was his ability to do things that no one else could do. At the end of the day, that is what a star is all about: the unexpected play, improvisation, creativity. When you expect him to go one way, then he goes the other. This is what makes Neymar so special. The defender is convinced that he is going left and yet somehow from nowhere Neymar will flick the ball over the defender's head.

'He improvises and does not follow the established rules of football. In the beginning, I watched him closely; I wanted to see how far he could go. Well ... every day he would create something new. The end result is that we haven't seen everything Neymar is capable of.'

What are his best qualities?
'His imagination; he manages to get out of situations which no one would bet on. One thing he needs to improve on is his passing, the quick one-touch passing at which Barcelona excel. His statistics were not brilliant in this area when he was at Santos. He would make mistakes in midfield. I told him that he must improve on that as it was fundamental for the team he was going to. On the edge of the box, what can I say, Neymar is in his element here.'

And his worst quality?

'His choice of music. When he goes into the changing rooms, he puts on that horrible funk, pagode, music, which I hate. It makes a right din. The music on the bus for away matches or before entering the pitch. I must have told him a million times to turn the volume down or to switch it off. But he just does not listen. In the changing rooms, he is always dancing, talking, joking with his teammates. It does not seem like he is about to play an important match. It does not matter if it's the Libertadores final or a league match, Neymar is playing football just like he did on the beach or in the street. It is fun time. His happiness is contagious.'

And you have paid the price for this happiness on more than one occasion …

'When we became champions, the lads kept throwing water at me and Neymar was the instigator. Then there was the egg in the face for my birthday incident. The lads just kept throwing eggs, flower and water and laughed non-stop. But this is normal in a team. Neymar is very polite compared to some of the players nowadays.'

But he is still a kid?

'Yes. He is still a kid like the others. He goes to clubs, hangs out with girls and does the things kids do at that age but, compared to certain others, he is respectful and polite. He turns up to training and shakes your hand and says 'hi' to everyone at all levels in the club.

'He is very friendly with people. His hair, his clothes and his practical jokes made people think he was a bit of a rebel but they were wrong; he is a kid with his feet firmly on the ground who always listens to his father, his trainers and his physio.

'He is completely focused on his job. I'll give you

an example: my flat was at the training centre in Santos. Sometimes I would wake up at two or three in the morning and his car was in the car park. He had just finished a TV advert in São Paulo or Rio and instead of sleeping at home with his mother and father, he would come straight to the club so that he could start his day's work. He would have breakfast and then go straight to training. No one asked him to, he just did it because he is a professional.

'Another example: in March 2013, the Brazilian national team was playing in Europe: first in Switzerland, then in London. We were playing a league match in south Brazil. Neymar managed to get back the same day and played. He was the best player on the pitch. He is not like lots of other footballers who complain all the time: "Coach, it hurts here, there, etc.". He never says he is hurting.'

And yet he gets lots of knocks?
'That's true but he never gets injured. He has never had a serious injury. Why? Because he is very strong, physically. In Brazil, we play on a Sunday. Those that play on Sunday do not train on Monday. But Neymar was always there, ready to take instructions from the trainer. He was never tired, he was always fit and his medicals were the best of the team. He has an excellent aerobic stamina, which is rare for a striker, who does not need it as much as a midfielder or winger; all a striker needs is speed and acceleration. But Neymar recovers very quickly from physical effort. He can string moves together without having to stop.'

A professional who is physically strong, polite, responsible, gifted with improvisation … There must have been something other than the music which made you worry about him?
'The thing that worried me the most was his non-footballing

commitments. They kept increasing and for me there were too many. Yes, he was young and, yes, he handled it well, but there comes a point where it gets too much and it tires you out. How long could he keep going like that? I spoke to him about it a lot and also with his father, as we were worried. We were worried he would burn out and that his image was being exploited too much.'

In terms of his image, how did he become such a world phenomenon in such a short time?

'I think he became so famous so quickly because he conveys happiness, he gives you the joy of playing football that any kid has. Neymar is the image of someone who is always happy, never complaining; a boy who enjoys himself on and off the pitch, who changes his look all the time, a message which strikes a chord with the entire world.

'We landed in Japan once to play the Club World Cup and it was unbelievable the attention he received. We played all over Brazil and the airports were always full of kids. Everyone wanted the Mohican and everyone wanted to be like him. Neymar is aware of this and knows he has a responsibility towards his fans and he knows how to dedicate himself to his people. He does not hold back when there are autographs to sign and photos to be taken.'

One moment, one match, one goal, one special memory of your time with Neymar?

'The moment that has etched itself in my heart is not on the pitch but when he became a father. We were leaving for Manizales in Colombia to play against Once Caldas in the Libertadores. I met him in the lift and he was looking sad, which I thought was strange. "What's the matter?" I asked, and he said, "No ... I've done something that I shouldn't have, something bad, I've got a girl pregnant."

'I reassured him: "Being a father is the most important thing in the world; the most beautiful thing in the world." I was scared and concerned as I had never seen him like this before and right before an important match.

'I continued to reassure him: "There's no need to worry, no need to be sad, you should be happy." He started to lighten up and he walked out of the lift with a more serene face than when he'd got in. I went to see the baby, I met the mother. David Lucca has been to training with me. It was important to me. I am also a father to three kids. I think becoming a father has made Neymar grow up quicker.'

Let's talk about the [2013] Confederations Cup: Did Neymar's performance surprise you?
'No, not at all. A few weeks earlier, before the cup, I spoke to his father. I always spoke to his father when there was a problem. The problem was his future: should he stay with Santos, go to Barcelona or go to Madrid. He needed to make the next step in his life and this really started to weigh him down. He did not show it but I could see it, I could see he was not himself.

'The fans did not mince their words, they told him what they felt; insults flew from the stands. So much so that Neymar started to feel uncomfortable at Santos. He was also not playing particularly well for Brazil.

'The day before the official announcement, when the deal with Barcelona was done, he came to training and called me. I could see he was different. "What's the matter?" I asked. Neymar said, "Profe it's over. I signed the contract last night." He was happy. I gave him a hug and told him that I was happy for him. I knew how important it was for him.

He had lifted a great weight from his shoulders. He felt relieved and I believe that it was for this reason that he played the Confederations Cup he played.'

To finish, who is Neymar in two words?
'He is a fantastic player who is different to all the others. As a coach, I see it like this: there are different, special, players and there are good players. He is in the first category. Apart from that, I believe that for a player to be different from the other players, he has to be a good person. He is that. In two or three years, he will be the best player in the world.'

Will he overtake Messi?
'It is difficult to say but he will reach Messi's level. It will happen gradually and naturally, like a handing over, as happened with Ronaldinho and Messi. Neymar is preparing himself for this role. His objectives are clear and he will achieve them. He is not the sort of player who thinks if things go well then that's fine but if they go badly then that's fine too. He wants to be the best player in the world. He does not talk about it but he thinks about it. I know this is the case. He has the personality to do it.'

Chapter 23

Remake

You know John Wayne? And his gallery of Wild West characters? Ringo Kid, Ethan Edwards, Rooster Cogburn aka 'El Grinta', Colonel York, John Bernard Books, the Shootist. All of them hard as a rock. Take Grinta, who, with his Winchester in one hand and his Colt in the other, galloping on horseback with the reins in his mouth, could take on four bandits and knock them off – even with one eye missing, a bit overweight and tipsy on whiskey.

True Grit – what a film! John Wayne won his only Oscar for that film in 1970. (And the Coen brothers remade it in 2010, with Jeff Bridges in the John Wayne role.) So what have the Old West and the Duke got to do with Neymar Jr? Well, according to João Paulo de Jesus Lopes, the best man to stop Neymar in his tracks is John Wayne. The vice-chairman of São Paulo Football Club made this humorous remark on a Paulista radio station in April 2012. A joke – but only just. The vice-chairman knew there was truth behind his words, as his team had just been brutally beaten by Santos in the Paulista semi-finals for the third year running. Neymar had scored three goals in the match and no one managed to get close to him.

It was on 29 April, in a match in Morumbi. Santos were in light blue, São Paulo in white. Before the spectators had even sat down, it was 1–0 to Santos. In the third minute, Alan Kardec received the ball in the area and Paulo Miranda brought him down. Referee Paulo Cesar de Oliveira blew for a penalty. Neymar took it: a long run-up and he slammed it into the top corner. No chance for Denis. It was Neymar's 100th goal for Santos. Three years and 50 days had passed since his debut with Peixe on 7 March 2009 and Neymar Jr had already joined the elite group of Santos goalscorers.

Neymar's 100th goal in official competitions had come three months earlier, on the day of his twentieth birthday, 5 February 2012, against Palmeiras in the Presidente Prudente Stadium: a header to register his first goal of the year and the 100th of his career. Of those, 82 were with Santos, eight with the Brazil senior side, nine with the Under-20s and one with the Under-17s.

O Globo examined his track record: 70 had come from his right foot, 21 from his left foot, seven from his head, one was scored with his shoulder and one with his chest. Seventy-two goals had come from within the area, ten from outside the area, sixteen from penalties and two from free kicks.

The newspaper outlined the goalscoring progress made by Neymar: fifteen goals in his first professional season (2009), 44 in 2010 and 40 in 2011. But it was not just statistics: comparisons with other players were made.

Messi, for example, achieved his 100th goal at 22 years and three months. Ronaldo, on the other hand, achieved his century a little earlier than Neymar: 'O Fenómeno' scored his 100th goal when he was nineteen years and four days old. Pelé was only seventeen years and nine months – but he had become a professional footballer at fifteen. The milestone of 100 goals is a useful tool for journalists in Brazil to compare Messi to Neymar – albeit that it is not a fair comparison, as there is an abyss between the football played by the Argentinian and that played by the Brazilian. And Messi is a three times winner of the Ballon d'Or. But nevertheless, Neymar reached his 100th goal before Messi.

Carrying on, we come to Neymar's 101st goal with Santos, which was like a ripe pear ready to fall from the tree. It came in the 31st minute of the semi-final match against São Paulo. Rodolfo, the Tricolour number 3, failed to clear properly. The ball landed at Ganso's feet and he threaded the ball to Neymar. The number 11 skipped past Miranda and, as Denis came off his line, Neymar fired the ball into the bottom left corner.

This prompted the first remake of the series: Neymar Jr danced the corner flag dance of Jorge dos Santos Filho, aka Juary. Juary was a Santos striker who went on to play in Europe in the early 1980s, first in Italy (Avellino, Inter, Ascoli and Cremonese) then in Portugal. In 1978, at Morumbi against São Paulo, Juary scored and then celebrated with his now famous dance.

For Neymar, it was not only a call back to that famous dance, it was a tribute to Juary's 101 goals scored in four seasons with Santos (1976–79 and 1989).

In the second half, Neymar made it 3–1 and Santos fell back. Neymar went over the top with flowery dribbling and dramatic falls (Emerson Leão, the Tricolour coach, advised Neymar at the end of the match to not repeat such a show of tricks and skills when playing for Brazil), but the end result was the desired one. Peixe was in the final of the Paulistão for the fourth year running.

In the first of those years, 2009, their attempt failed as they lost to Ronaldo's Corinthians. But in 2010 and 2011 they won the title, against Santo André and *Timão* respectively. Now they had the chance to bring home the club's 20th state title and be champions for the third year in a row.

The first leg was scheduled for 6 May: an away match against Guarani in Morumbi. A goal from Ganso and two from Neymar settled it. Santos's number 11 celebrated his first goal of the match with a remake of Serginho Chulapa's celebrations. He ran along the goal line, wobbled as though running out of breath and then collapsed to the ground: Chulapa, who played for Santos as a striker in 1983-84, 1986 and 1990, had celebrated in this way when he scored the goal that won Peixe the Paulistão in 1984.

The kid from Mogi das Cruzes took his tally to 105 with the second goal against Guarani. He overtook Serginho Chulapa and João Paulo (1977–84, 1992) to become the best goalscorer in the post-Pelé era. Neymar was pleased to have reached another milestone.

O Chulapa did not mind that his record had been broken: 'I am not jealous of my record, especially as it was Neymar who broke it. He is only 20 and still needs to develop. We are expecting a lot from him. I was choked with emotion seeing him score that goal and pay tribute to me. It is nice to see that Neymar remembers the history of the club he loves and acknowledges the work we have done. I cannot wait for next Sunday. The second leg of the final.'

The *Globoesporte* reported on the second leg of the final and a day of celebration – of Santos's centenary and third Paulistão in a row, marked by three goals from Neymar:

'We used to listen to our parents and grandparents tell us the story of the future of Pelé at Santos; now we have to add the story of Neymar at Santos. It is a story which has a new chapter as of this Sunday 13 May 2012.

'Neymar's Santos won 4–2 against Guarani and claimed its third Paulista league in a row. Something no one else has been able to achieve since Pelé's Santos of 1967, 1968 and 1969.'

The black commemorative T-shirt bore the legend *Não canso de ser tri. Campeonato paulista 2010 2011 2012* ('I never tire of three. Paulista league 2010, 2011 and 2012') . Neymar was wearing it on the stage. On his head, another tribute: a white headband with the words '100 per cent Jesus' on it. He ran round the pitch, dribbled round TV cameras and photographers. He shouted 'Olé' at each slalom. In the stands, the fans started laughing.

The celebrations at Morumbi carried on. Neymar was in his pants; the only other bit of clothing he was wearing was his headband. The party had only just begun. Back at Santos, the team had a meal together in a *churrasqueria* and then on to the club. Neymar took his white Porsche to the club and was one of the first to arrive.

In the nightclub, 'Neymarzetes', there was a free bar and an exclusive guest list. The DJ cranked up the tunes and there were two bands as well, Batukada and Revelação, funk and pagode music. Neymar got on the stage and sang '*Eu sou o cara pra você*' ('I am the guy for you'), a song by his singer friend, Thiaguinho. At 5.30am the party ended.

The party for the Brasilerão awards ceremony, on 3 December 2012, in the HSBC Brazil hall in São Paulo, was more contained. The show was dominated by Fluminense, who won the national league title, and Fred, who took home three trophies. In 2011, Neymar, sporting his grey gilet, white shirt and red tie, had been voted best player in the league but this year he had to make do with the best striker award and the *Globolinha*, the award given for the best goal: this was for the number 11's goal scored against Atlético-MG on 17 October, on Neymar's 200th appearance for Santos. Neymar received a hearty round of applause when he took the stage. He accepted the trophy and said, 'It is a great season, the best of my career.' He had scored 43 goals, won a historic third consecutive Paulistão and the Recopa Sul-Americana (won in September against Universidad de Chile) with Santos, and taken a whole host of individual awards including 'best player in the Americas', a title bestowed on Neymar by the Uruguayan newspaper *El País* for the second year running.

A great year indeed but there was a gaping hole. Not in the Brasilerão, although Santos finished in eighth place, nor in the Libertadores, where Santos exited in the semi-finals against Corinthians, but in the 2012 Olympics. Brazil had never won the Olympic gold medal: it was, and remains, the only trophy Brazil have not won. Many greats have tried – Ronaldo, Rivaldo, Bebeto – but none has succeeded. Ronaldinho tried at the Beijing Olympics in 2008 but it did not work out and in the end he was consoled by Messi after Argentina thrashed Brazil 3–0 in the semi-finals.

In London it seemed like the heavens were aligning. Mano Menezes called on all the young talent for the London Olympics: Neymar, Paulo Henrique, Lucas, Oscar, Pato, Rafael da Silva; and he strengthened the team with three champions: Thiago Silva, Marcelo and Hulk. On paper, Brazil looked as though they had it in the bag.

The road to Wembley started on 26 July 2012 against Egypt in the Millennium Stadium in Cardiff. Brazil put on a fantastic show for the fans and were 3–0 up after half an hour, Neymar scoring the third with a header. In the second half, Egypt clawed two back and the atmosphere was tense right until the end.

The other two countries in Group C were Belarus and New Zealand. At Old Trafford, against Belarus, Brazil were a goal down but then Neymar provided an assist for Pato before himself converting a free kick. A third goal came via a flick of the heel from Oscar. New Zealand were next. Brazil were already through but won this game too, 3–0, without breaking sweat.

In the quarter-finals it was Honduras; Brazil won 3–2. And the semi-final against South Korea was a relative breeze: 3–0. Brazil were in the final for the first time since 1988.

Neymar had been immense throughout the five matches, with three goals and four assists. He was the second highest scorer in the team, Leandro Damião taking first place with six goals. Neymar was happy but said that his role was to do the best for Brazil, like all the other players, and help win the gold medal. He said he had not slept after the semi-final against South Korea but he had no problems with sleep now; however, he thought he might go without a night's sleep if Brazil managed to win the gold.

Neymar was to get his sleep, though. On 11 August 2012, Mexico won the final and denied Brazil the gold medal they were so desperate to win. Oribe Peralta was man of the match at Wembley Stadium. He scored in the 28th second of the match following an unbelievable mistake from Rafael and Brazil went to pieces. In the first half, they got nowhere. In the second half, they got going again and Neymar got the best chance: a good move from Oscar and the ball was about 10 metres from the goal on the left side but Neymar spooned the ball over the bar.

Peralta, the Mexican number 9, put the final nail in the coffin in the 75th minute. Unmarked in the area, he headed in for 2–0. Hulk pulled one back in the first minute of injury time but it was too late. Mexico had won the gold medal and Brazil had lost a third Olympic final, following their failures in 1984 against France and in 1988 against the Soviet Union. While the Mexicans were celebrating, Neymar cried on the Wembley turf.

The next day the Brazilian newspapers had a field day.

They talked of a poor performance and a second debacle like the 2011 Copa America. Doubts were cast over the number 11's future ahead of the upcoming World Cup in Brazil. There was a lot to cry about ...

Chapter 24

Thanks all for everything

There are those who think Neymar should go to Europe this year.

There are those who think it would be better for him to wait until after the World Cup.

Those who think it would be a mistake to go.

Those who think it would be a fiasco.

Those who think he needs more experience.

Those who think he is not mature enough.

Those who think he should go to Real Madrid.

Those who think Barcelona would be better.

Those who love Pep Guardiola.

Those who think the Premier League is the best.

Those who say his head is in the clouds.

Those who say he is a national treasure.

Those who say he thinks more about his hair than his football.

Those who are sick and tired of him.

Those who do not care.

Those who only care about Santos.

Those who just want him to be happy.

Those who do not know what to say.

This was not an exaggeration. In the first five months of 2013, there were hundreds of opinions on what Neymar should do. The daily debate about Paulistão football and the national team (now managed by Luiz Felipe Scolari) was superseded by talk about Neymar.

Will or he won't he? Will he stay with Santos or will he choose one of the big European clubs who have been chasing him for years? Is it absolutely necessary for him to experience Europe?

Neymar was bombarded with questions until he felt nauseous. His response was more or less the same every time.

For example, on 4 March 2013, Neymar Jr was a guest on the TV show *Programa do Jô* on the Globo Network (a US-style, David Letterman-style talk show).

Jô Soares, the presenter, a larger-than-life and highly entertaining figure, greeted Neymar with a hug and a kiss. He asked him to take off his black baseball cap to see his haircut: a peroxide tuft in the style of Marilyn Monroe, which got a few giggles from the 'Neymarzetes' (Neymar's young, female fans) in the audience.

The chat started. Not even five minutes had passed and there it was: the question of all questions. Soares launched into it: 'Everyone asks me, everyone is asking themselves, when are you going to Europe, before or after the World Cup? It looks like Barcelona has given an advance as a guarantee. Can you comment on that or are you not allowed?' Neymar smiled and said, 'I have been answering this question for years. I am happy at Santos and I want to see out my contract to the end of next year when it expires. Of course, I dream of going to Europe. It is the dream of any young boy, any footballer. But everyone has their time. Some go very young, others later. My moment has not yet come.'

Jô Soares was not deterred and kept pressing for an answer: 'But if you went to Europe which team would you like to play for?' Neymar was vague in his answer: 'There is not a team I would like to play for in particular ...' Soares was not for letting up: 'Don't lie to me, boy, a bit of respect please.' Neymar laughed and tried another well-used tactic: 'When I was a little boy, I played a lot with my Playstation and, just like lots of my friends, I put my name in the Barcelona, Real Madrid and Chelsea teams. I didn't have a favourite team as my idols played for different teams and I liked all of them.'

Jô was not satisfied and he kept banging the drum: 'Real Madrid or Barcelona?' Neymar laughed nervously but kept his nerve: 'They are two great clubs.' The anchor was not giving in that easily: 'Perhaps Bayern Munich, where Guardiola is going.' Juninho came straight back: 'Another great club and a great coach.'

Jô Soares looked him straight in the eye and asked, 'Are you a footballer or a politician?' The audience laughed raucously.

He was not a politician but he did not deviate from the script. He had learned his part and repeated it about ten days later in a TV interview with *Esporte Espetacular*.

Neymar was not budging. Without blushing, Neymar confirmed he was going out with Bruna Marquezine, a seventeen-year-old actress born in Duque de Caxias, a city in the state of Rio de Janeiro, famous for acting the role of 'Salete' in the TV soap *Mulheres Apaixonadas*. (This love story was to end on 11 February 2014 – not even a year. Bruna confirmed the end of the romance in a press conference. The reason given for the break-up was the long distance, once Neymar was in Spain. The actress deleted all her photos of Neymar from her social media pages.)

Neymar was happy to talk about it and explained that they had no intention of hiding from the paparazzi. A hint about where he was going in the future? Nothing doing. He was as quiet as a mouse.

In the bars, the stadium, on TV, the fans, critics and journalists, professional footballers and ex-pros could not stop talking about it.

Pelé argued that it was not Neymar's age that was the problem but his maturity and physical condition. In England, Italy and Germany, the game was played hard. The referees let things flow more. You needed to have experience to play in the European leagues and at that level. O Rei said that Santos needed Neymar and that therefore it would be better if he stayed, but if he wanted to go, he should go to Barcelona; it was perfect for him. And, just for good measure, he gave another piece of advice to the young Neymar: he said he should worry less about his hairstyle and more about his football.

Ronaldo, on the other hand, told him to go: 'If a Brazilian player does not weigh himself up against the European leagues, he will not be a complete player.'

Romario, the ex-Barcelona player, now a federal politician in Brasilia, could not see a reason for Neymar to go, other than a financial reason. He said the Spanish league was easier than the Brazilian league. He thought Neymar would not learn much playing in Europe.

Walter Casagrande Junior, the 50-year-old former centre forward for Corinthians, Torino and Ascoli, now a commentator for Globo Network, confessed that he had changed his mind on the matter. Sitting on the steps of the Nyon stadium in Switzerland, where Brazil were training ahead of a friendly against Italy in March 2013, Casagrande Junior explained, 'I have always thought Neymar should stay in Brazil as he had no need to go to Europe, but today I believe that he has reached the top in Brazilian football. He needs that international experience. He has to play in a more challenging league like the Spanish *Liga*, the English Premier League or the Italian *Serie A*. He needs to go now. He will be a lot better prepared for the 2014 World Cup.'

The view of one of the great Brazilian opinionists was completely the opposite: Juca Kfouri, the editor of *Folha* in São Paulo, commented, 'No. I am not one of those who believes that he should play in Europe. For me, this is the conformist position. Football in our country should create the conditions where Neymar can stay in Brazil.

'The Brazil team has won three World Cups, 1958, 1962 and 1970, with a team that was made of players that played in the Brazilian leagues. Things have changed since then. The world is global and so is football. But I believe that today with our economic boom compared to the European economic crisis, we have the chance to keep our players here. It is not just by chance that in the last few years, more than 1,100 players have come home, reversing the trend which had been in place for some time. There is more money in football. Just think, the earnings of the top 100 Brazilian clubs have surpassed US$396 million in 2003 and US$1,400 million in 2012. The Corinthians saw their income grow by 481 per cent whereas Santos has reached a record of 548 per cent. It is a crying shame that the CBF has put in place a policy which is harmful to the interests of football in our country. The CBF has focused for years on transforming the national team but has put the development of club football, like Pelé's Santos, Garrincha's Botafogo, Corinthians and Zico's Flamengo, on the back burner. When you go into a sports shop today, you find the Brazil top, but you also find the shirt for Bayern, Milan, Barcelona, Manchester United and even Boca or River but not those of our clubs. If a player like Neymar were to stay in Brazil, he could raise the level of our tournaments, our football and he could help sell it all over the world.'

The views were varied and all documented. However, the debate was not just limited to the question of Europe, and when Neymar might go. The player was also under fire. And it was not just Pelé who was giving him a ticking off. Many thought that, after three fabulous seasons, his performances were going downhill. Neymar was not shining so bright any more, either for Santos or Brazil. He was agitated; he fought with the referees, who he felt did not look out for him; he argued with opposition defenders who marked him too closely; he scored fewer goals. Why?

The assumptions and interpretations were varied. It started because Neymar turned himself into a pop star. He appeared on TV, he went out with girls who ended up on the cover of magazines, he attended parties, the lot; Neymar Jr had entered the world of showbiz. And that was not all.

The thirteen sponsors he had racked up wanted their piece of the action and required him to attend events and promos and to make TV advertisements. Neymar, at only 21, had the world at his feet. The list of clubs that were knocking on his door with offers was enough to make you dizzy, and it grew longer every day: from Barcelona to Chelsea; from Real Madrid to Manchester City. Some were prepared to go to great lengths to get the star on their team. How can someone possibly concentrate on football when all that is going on in the background?

Every time Neymar agreed to an interview, he denied that he was distracted by the questions around his future. He said you could not have 10 out of 10 on your school record all of the time. Sometimes you had a bad day and a bad match to boot.

A missed goal opportunity would be interpreted as a sign that Neymar was not fully focused on football or Santos, and therefore he wanted to go. A goal scored would be cited as evidence that it was too easy for him, so he needed to go, and it was better he left now.

The pressure was immense. The constant questioning and commentary around his future was enough to tire anyone. On top of that, Santos was not working out. Neymar had lost his great friend, Paulo Henrique. Ganso had left for São Paulo.

The emotion was clear for all to see when the two met as rivals for the first time on 3 February 2013 at Vila Belmiro. Neymar's reaction to the Santos fans who wolf-whistled Ganso, accused him of being a mercenary, threw coins at him and tried to attack him, was unforgettable: he defended his friend and asked the fans to keep calm.

Walter Montillo, the Argentinian Santos had bought from Cruzeiro to replace Paulo Henrique, did not achieve the level of performance that Ramalho expected.

Santos could not get into gear. Peixe were suffering, but still progressing in the Paulistão. In the quarter-finals they managed to beat Palmeiras on penalties. The same against Mogi Mirim in the semi-finals. Santos scraped through to the Paulistão final for the fifth year running.

Neymar had scored twelve goals, one less than the leading goalscorer for the tournament, Ponte Preta's William, but he did not manage to score in the quarters or the semis.

Nor the final.

The first leg at Pacaembu on 12 May ended 2–1 to Corinthians. The second leg, seven days later in Vila Belmiro, was a 1–1 draw, with Cicero and Danilo scoring. Santos's dreams were dashed. It would have been a new record for Peixe and the Paulistão. The fans were left with the bitter-sweet taste of an historic victory that had slipped through their hands, and the shame of seeing the Corinthians' fans celebrate in their stadium. It was not a good day for Neymar. He was nervous and argumentative. He lost the ball fourteen times (out of 40 balls received) and ended the game without having had one shot on goal.

The newspapers wrote that Neymar had spent the last week negotiating with Barcelona. Everyone believed that this would be the last final that he would play for Santos. Those in the know about Neymar's future were convinced that the agreement would be signed within the week. The countdown of matches began: 22 May against Joinville in the Brazil Cup; 26 May against Flamengo in the first round of Brasilerão matches.

The cup match at Vila Belmiro was played under a downpour and ended 0–0; Santos went through thanks to the advantage they had from the first leg. Neymar played well but did not score. It was his seventh match without a goal.

The night before the game, at the Paulista Federation party, Neymar had been voted the 'Paulistão star' for the fourth year running. When the smartly dressed Santos forward walked off the stage with the trophy in his hand, *Lance* asked the question for the umpteenth time. Neymar calmly replied that his future was here and that he was staying with Santos. He added, 'A new championship [the Brasilerão] starts and I hope we can win it.'

On Friday 24 May, Neymar visited the offices of NR Sport at Santos HQ. He talked with his father and Wagner Ribeiro before reaching Vila Belmiro. On the chairman's desk were two offers: one from Real Madrid and one from Barcelona. When he left the stadium at one in the morning, there were lots of people and TV cameras waiting for father and son. Neymar Pai spoke first: 'I will speak with my son and we will decide together. We will try and help Santos as best we can.'

Neymar, looking tired, said, 'We are going home to rest.

We will decide what is best with a clear head. I am pleased about the offers from these two great clubs.'

The next day, Juninho went to the CT Rei Pelé and, before training, he told the coach and his teammates that a decision had been reached. He was going to Barcelona. Neymar then tied a camera to his head and filmed what would be his last session with Santos.

At the end of training, Neymar wrote on the walls of the changing rooms '*Eu Vou' Mas ... Eu Volto!*' (I am going but I'll be back!). A helicopter was waiting to take him to a resort on Tabatinga beach in Caraguatatuba on the São Paulo coast. He was best man at Paulo Henrique's wedding. The ex-Santos number 10 was marrying Giovanna Costi.

Neymar posed with the newlyweds for the customary photos. He was wearing a grey suit with a light blue tie. Later, Neymar got on the stage and entertained alongside singer Diego Faria. He did not shy away from dancing either and got down to '*Elas ficam Loucas*'. At the end of the party, Neymar headed to Brasilia where he would be playing his last match with Santos in the Mané Garrincha Stadium.

But first he sent a farewell letter to his fans via Twitter, Facebook and Instagram. It was ten in the evening on 25 May 2013:

'I am here with family and friends who are helping me write these words ... I cannot wait until Monday ... My family and friends know what my decision is. On Monday I will sign for Barcelona. I want to thank all the Santos fans for these nine incredible years. My feelings for the club and the fans will never die. They are eternal! Only a club like Santos could give me all that I have had both on and off the pitch. I am grateful to the Peixe fans who have supported me, even in hard times. Titles, goals, dribbling, celebrations and songs that the fans have created for me will be with me forever in my heart ... I shall play the match in Brasilia tomorrow.

'I want one last chance to play for Santos and hear the fans shout my name ... as the anthem goes, it is an honour that not everyone can have. It is a strange time for me, sad (to say goodbye) and happy (for the new challenge ahead). God bless my choice ... I will always be Santos!!'

On Sunday 26 May, at 4.00pm in the new Mané Garrincha Stadium in Brasilia (a stadium built for the 2014 World Cup), the first round of Brasilerão matches got under way and the last act of Neymar's adventure with Santos began. Nine years after arriving at Peixe, five years after his debut in the famous white shirt, and now with 229 matches played, 138 goals scored and six titles won (three Paulistão, one Brazil Cup, one Libertadores and one Recopa Sul-Americana), Neymar da Silva Santos said goodbye to the club that had seen him grow up.

The match was a sell-out: 63,501 spectators for a total gate of 6,948,710 reais – a record in the history of Brazilian football. The ratings for the live broadcast via Globo Network were higher than ever before. It was an emotional and tearful Sunday.

In the changing rooms before the match, Neymar, next to Rafael and Victor Andrade, formed a circle with his teammates and, with tears rolling down his face, he said, 'I want to thank all of you for the moments we've had together, the training sessions, the victories and the titles. It is not easy for me to leave you but I am living my dream. I wanted to play today to have one last chance to play 90 minutes with you, irrespective of whether we win or lose. Thank you all for everything. I will always be your fan and I wish you all the best. I will always be your friend who will support you, wherever I may be.'

The national anthem boomed around the stadium and the emotion rose up within Neymar. More tears. It was time for the match to get under way and Neymar passed the ball for his last kick-off. The match finished 0–0 and Neymar could not manage a goal. Afterwards, at the edge of the pitch, Neymar sat with a Flamengo shirt around his shoulders, clearly choked with emotion. He thanked the fans and when he was asked what it would be like playing with Messi, he replied, 'Playing with Messi, Iniesta and Xavi is a great honour. Dani Alves, as well, he kept telling me to go to Barcelona.'

That evening, on *Domingão do Faustão,* Neymar spoke about his decision to go to the Catalan club: 'Every kid has a dream. Some dream of becoming a footballer, others a dentist or a reporter. I had one dream: I wanted to become a professional footballer. I've done it. Today, Barcelona is letting me live the dream of a young kid with the face of a man, I am a father after all. The dream of playing for a club like that is amazing.'

Chapter 25

Number 11s

A conversation with José Macia, aka Pepe

'Three or four times in my career, I had the chance to go to Barcelona, but I always preferred staying here at Santos. I have no regrets but I do often wonder what life would have been like if I had accepted that offer. Would my financial situation have been better? I'll never know. But the doubt lingers. Neymar was right to go when he did. If he'd stayed at Santos, he would have always had that nagging doubt about what his future would have been like in Europe.'

José Macia, better known as Pepe, class of 1935, son of Spanish immigrants from Galicia, is the second highest goalscorer in the history of Santos: 405 goals in 750 matches – even if Macia claims he is number one, as Pelé, with his 1,901 goals, 'does not count. He came from another planet, from Saturn'.

In his long career, Pepe won everything there was to win: 51 domestic and international titles, including two World Cups (1958 and 1962). Wearing the number 11 shirt for Santos, *O Canhão da Vila*, 'the Cannon at Vila Belmiro' (a nickname he got from Ernani Franco, an announcer for Radio Atlantica, for his missile-like shots which reached speeds of 122km/h), played for fifteen years from 1954 to 1969. He was left-footed, quick and agile. He was one of the forwards who stunned the world and in Baixada Santista his is one of the names still remembered off by heart: Dorval, Mengálvio, Coutinho, Pelé and Pepe.

On 3 May 1969, he said his farewells to professional football on the pitch and became a manager: Brazil, Portugal, Peru, Saudi Arabia, Japan and Qatar, where, at Al Ahli in 2004/05, he coached a certain Pep Guardiola.

Today he is here to talk about Neymar, Barcelona and Peixe in his house in Ponta da Praia in Santos. In a mix of Spanish and Portuguese, he remembers the electrifying tournaments of the 1950s and 1960s at Camp Nou, where Santos played Barcelona three times: winning 1–5 in 1959, losing 4–3 in 1960 with Pepe scoring two of the goals and losing again, 2–0, in 1963.

Having seen Pepe in action, the Spanish club wanted to bring him into their team at all costs. They did not succeed. But many years later they succeeded in attracting another Santos number 11: Neymar.

'He made the right decision. Playing for the best team in the world in one of the best leagues in Europe and to be surrounded by the best can't be wrong.'

But does it not upset you to see him playing in a Barcelona shirt, when you didn't manage it?
'Sure. It is weird after all these years to see Neymar in the famous *Blaugrana* shirt. I would have liked him to stay in Brazil a bit longer but modern football is like that. The numbers involved are so high that you have to accept what a player and the market decides. I am a fan of Neymar's, and have been right from when he was a young boy; I think it is the right thing to go to Europe.'

When did you meet him?
'I met him when he played for the youth teams in Santos.

I saw him for the first time in a futsal match. The final score was 2–0 and Neymar scored both goals. He was the smallest player in the team but his tricks were incredible.'

Since then he has come on a lot …
'Yes. Neymar has grown into a mature player, the best in Brazilian football today. A success that has not surprised me. He is a mature boy and he is responsible, with his feet on the ground; he has always known how to make the right decisions and listen to the advice of his father.'

How far do you think he can go?
'That's a tricky question. Messi is unarguably the best player in the world right now but Neymar can learn from him and I believe that in time, he will show Europe the same things he has shown here in Brazil. In the next two or three years, the title of best player will be between Neymar and Messi.'

From someone who has played with the greatest Brazilian players, who would you compare Neymar to?
'For me, Pelé and Garrincha were the best players of all time and are still the best to this day. They won everything there is to win and displayed such beauty in their dribbling and elegance in their goals. I remember in 1969, the last year I played for Santos, Pelé was still able to invent new things which I had never seen before. Neymar is Neymar; he does not have the characteristics of Pelé or Garrincha, but he does have creativity, imagination and lightning speed in common with them.'

And yet, you said that Neymar would have been on the bench when Pelé was playing for Santos …
Pepe smiles. 'Yes. I did say that. It was because Dorval,

Mengálvio, Coutinho, Pepe and Pelé were a formation that made history with Santos. Who knows, Neymar might have got on in the second half for a few minutes, or we could have tried to convince Lula [the manager at the time] to put six forwards on the pitch. It would have been hard for Neymar to earn the number 11 shirt – I would not have given him mine without a fight … It would have been a good fight as well.' Pepe bursts out laughing at this point.

From number 11 to number 11, what do you appreciate about the young Neymar?
'Two things: his nifty dribbling in close quarters and his nerves of steel in front of goal. In a tiny space, Neymar is able to jump and skip around his marker, a skill he picked up from futsal. I was fast, but I needed space to free myself of my marker. I played on the left side, a bit like Cristiano Ronaldo does today. When I was in the area or up front on my own against the last defender, I always opted for the hard shot. Neymar, on the other hand, manages to dribble past the goalkeeper or trick him with a lob. Another thing is that, although he is right footed, he scores great goals with his left as well. I, on the other hand, am left-footed and out of my 430 goals scored, only four were with my right foot. We have the ability to execute perfect free-kicks. Neymar has a more varied repertoire; mine were just brute force.'

(You did not want to get in the way of the ball. The story goes that at the end of the 1950s, the São Paulo player Alfredo Ramos, 'O Polvo', was in the wall and on the receiving end of a Pepe missile and ended up on the floor, KO'd. He took more than twenty minutes to come round.)

Let's stick with Santos. How important was Neymar?
'He was fundamental. He was instrumental to Santos in the

four years he was here. The team was different when he played and when he didn't you could tell. Without Neymar, Santos was less of an opponent. When he was playing, Santos always had a chance of winning. I am not saying he was like Pelé but ... and then Pelé, unlike Neymar, had a great team around him. I do not want to boast but, with Milan, in the second half of the 1963 Intercontinental Cup, Pelé did not play, but I did, and scored two crucial goals.'

Let's change topic. Let's talk about Brazil and the 2014 World Cup.
'The Brazilian team played a brilliant Confederations Cup and upped its play and its productivity. Step by step, just like Felipão [Luiz Felipe Scolari] said. It is a team that has exceptional players, Neymar not included. It is well structured and they gelled their way of playing. It does not grab me but everyone has their own view. One thing is clear: with the World Cup on home turf, we are the favourites. Neymar will need to show that he is the best.'

Chapter 26
NRJ

You learn a lot walking up the four flights of stairs at the offices of NR Sports, housed in a white building with the black and yellow company logo on the façade at number 56, Avenida Ana Costa in Santos. Here, in these new offices opened in May 2013, a group of twenty manage the image, wealth, public relations and e-commerce for Neymar Junior's official products. The spiral staircase and green carpets are a nice summary of the career and brand of the prodigy. There are photos of his father wearing the União Mogi shirt, a portrait of his grandad Arnaldo (an amateur footballer), and a maxim which father and son repeat religiously before a game: 'Every weapon forged against you will fail, and you will condemn every language which judges you. This is the way of the servants of the Lord and their right. Oracle of the Lord.' Five of these words have been immortalised in one of Neymar's tattoos, together with 'Blessed' and the names of Nadine, Rafaela and David Lucca, and a cross with a crown and biblical verse (verses 24 and 27 of the letters to the Corinthians).

As you walk up the stairs, there are group photos taken with his futsal teams, trophies, boots, medals, the shirt he wore when he won the Libertadores, large photos and the covers of magazines seen by half the world: *Time* magazine ('Neymar, the Next Pelé'), *Select* ('Futebol arte'). Every step is a new phase of the player's life. At the top there are

Subbuteo players with Neymar's face, a 'Neymar Jr. Football Club' game by Gulliver and a doll reminiscent of Barbie's Ken with two Brazil kits and two pairs of boots, made by Cosmokids.

There is no doubt that Neymar sells. There are all sorts of products with his image on them, including notebooks, mobile phone covers, cups, cushions, puzzles, jeans, drinks, sportswear, football boots, model cars, scented sweets and whatever else you can think of.

Neymar is a magnet: he pulls in all the sponsors just like he attracts the Neymarzetes. There are fourteen businesses that have targeted Neymar since he started at Santos: Santander, Nike, Panasonic, Unilever, Claro, Red Bull, Lupo, Tenys Pé Baruel, AmBev, Bateris Heliar, Volkswagen, Guaraná, GSK and Mentos. These are the companies that have chosen Neymar as the man to represent their brand. It worked: in 2012, adverts starring Neymar appeared on TV 5,472 times.

And it still works: Takumi Kajisha, executive director for Panasonic Corporation, confirmed that seeing is believing: 'Our brand has become more popular thanks to Neymar. He has done wonders for us in Brazil and now, with his arrival at Barcelona, he can help us on a global scale because Barcelona is well known in Asia and Africa. Neymar, as our ambassador in these markets, can achieve even more than he already has done.'

The figures are impressive: according to *France Football*, in 2012 Neymar earned €20 million, 70 per cent of which was from sponsorship; a figure which put him at fifth best paid footballer in the world, just behind David Beckham (€36 million), Leo Messi (€35 million), Cristiano Ronaldo (€30 million) and Samuel Eto'o (€24 million). This fortune is managed by NR Sport, founded in 2006 by Neymar Pai and his wife Nadine. The group encompasses NN Administration to manage the finances, NN Store to manage e-commerce and sale of other Neymar-related products, and NN Participações to manage the star's investments.

At the helm of the group, Neymar Pai, with the help of lawyers, marketing experts and financial consultants, looks to invest the earnings of Juninho to 'provide for the future five or six generations of the da Silva Santos family'. The investments are in property, treasury bonds and shares in well-established companies. The risk profile is low because, according to Neymar Pai, 'Our objective is not to earn money on the markets.'

One thing is clear and that is that the 'NRJ' brand created by the PR agency Lodocca is going great guns, just like the motto *Ousadia y Alegria* ('courage and joy') which comes from a conversation with Neymar's best friend Thiaguinho, a former member of the band Exaltasamba. These words define his way of playing: the joy of being on the ball and the courage of attacking dribbling. Neymar had these words stitched into his boots on the eve of the 2011 *Copa America*; it also became the title of a Thiaguinho album in 2012.

According to *SportsPro* magazine, *NRJ: Ousadia y Alegria* represents the most lucrative and commercially valuable sports star on the planet. The magazine places Neymar in first place ahead of golfer Rory McIlroy, Lionel Messi and Usain Bolt. Neymar is an impressive media phenomenon both in terms of image and economic value. On the social networking sites, on TV, in music and even in comics he is there. He has thirteen million fans on Facebook, 8 million followers on Twitter and 2.5 million on Instagram. He has not reached Cristiano Ronaldo's figures yet (more than 64 million on Facebook) or Leo Messi's (50 million on Facebook) but he is on the right track. Neymar is a hyperactive user of social media, which can't but help. He always has a photo to post, a story to tell, a face to pull. He tweets nine times a day on average, which is decidedly higher than others like him.

Let's not forget his own language: *eh toiss* – 'we are the friends'. And what about music: his goal celebration dance moves to the music of '*Ai Se Eu Te Pego*' ('Ah, when I get my hands on you') by Michel Teló or '*Eu Quero Tchu Eu Quero Tchá*' ('I want you') by João Luca & Marcelo have gone viral on the internet and have led to the worldwide success of the two songs.

Neymar has been in telenovelas such as *Amor à vida* and *Malhação*, and in TV series like *Aline* on TV Globo, guest starring as himself. He did a similar guest appearance in the kids' program *Carrossel* for SBT, where he played the coach of a group of kids visiting Vila Belmiro with their teacher.

There is a Panini comic aimed at seven to eleven-year-olds called *Neymar Jr*. The first issue, titled '*Um Garoto de talento*' ('A talented kid') came out on 30 May 2013. It was illustrated by Mauricio de Sousa, creator of Mônica and Cebolinha: two characters who had mesmerised entire generations in Brazil. De Sousa had already done comics of Pelé and Ronaldinho; Neymar was the obvious next step. The comic depicts him with his Mohican hair and his surfboard, going on lots of adventures on the beach and on the pitch. He is with his friends and family too.

Allan Sieber is a comic artist as well but his comic strips are not aimed at younger readers: they are sarcastic, acerbic, with a hint of black humour; they hit hard against Brazilian society. His criticisms of Brazilian society effuse from his comics and books like *Tudo Mais ou Menos Verdade – O Jornalismo Investigativo, Tendencioso e Ficcional* ('All more or less true – investigative journalism, biased and fictional').

In Rio de Janeiro, at a showing of his artwork, the bulky

bearded Sieber, originally from Porto Alegre, does not hold back when talking about Neymar's image. He is deliberately provocative and heretical. He says that Neymar's success is down to being *O Cara* ('the face, the symbol') of the 'C' class Brazilian, or rather the class that is climbing up the social ladder in Brazil thanks to the economic boom of the last few years – but above all thanks to the availability of credit on deferred payment plans. Nike goods, Beat headphones and even plastic surgery that can be paid for in 30, 40 or 50 instalments. Sieber talks of 'A generation of young people, necking a bottle of red wine, consumers who love the aesthetics of rappers, bling-bling, designer clothes, TV series, funk, pagode and *sertanejo universitário* ('backcountry university') music, who dream of becoming Neymar one day, of earning gazillions and hanging out with TV actresses. A generation which is beginning to understand the insurmountable distance between their hopes and goals and the reality of achieving them. A generation which, like the entire country, after the dream of the World Cup and Olympics in 2016, could end up like the Titanic.'

On the subject of Neymar, football and consumerism, another artist, 52-year-old Leda Catunda from São Paulo, does not agree. His works on the white walls of the Museum of Modern Art in Rio de Janeiro are a collage of logos, shirts, numbers, colours and materials from the world of football. 'Santos', a piece from 2012, the biggest at the exhibition (3.4 metres by 4 metres) merges pictures of Pelé, Neymar, the Triple title and the Libertadores. It combines the club's shield, taken from a rug, with a piece of curtain from the Peixe showers. Catunda says of Neymar, 'He belongs to a new generation which places great emphasis on how you look and your image. Just think of his hair, his tattoos, his look and his clothing. He is nevertheless always polite, religious, friendly and available with the public. Kids identify with him and his colours because in a mass-market, standardised world, people need identity, a model to follow. Sport, and football in particular, offers a democratic opportunity to identify yourself with something which, here in Brazil, has the same role as religion.' He talks about consumer society and adds, 'It is normal and integral to this generation. The order is: work, earn and consume as much as possible. And consumerism in football is emotional, pure desire which is satisfied when you buy the brand which represents a value. There is no longer "beauty" in aesthetics, there is only freedom to choose what you want to buy. Everything is sold with a logo of a team or a footballing icon like Neymar.'

Francisco Bosco, a poet, writer and doctor in literary theory at the Federal University in Rio de Janeiro, is convinced that Neymar embodies 'the essence of South American footballing talent, the gift of football, the mystery that is dribbling – qualities which had been lost for some time.' Bosco goes on: 'This is why he is the "hope of a return to that golden era of football, a renaissance in Brazilian football after the fall from grace over the last ten years".' According to Bosco, off the pitch, Neymar 'shows a charisma which neither Messi has nor Ronaldinho had. You can only compare him to David Beckham and Cristiano Ronaldo. Yes, Neymar belongs to a globalised football and is a celebrity in his own right – something which, in Brazil, began in the 1990s with Ronaldo, O Fenómeno, the first Brazilian to represent a similar transformation. Neymar is going down this path. At Barcelona he will be skyrocketed to the absolute heights of stardom.'

A special day

Happiness, dream, heartfelt emotion, family, help, God, Messi, Messi again, and, once more, *Messi.*

These were the words that Neymar Jr repeated on 3 June 2013. At 6.40pm, he appeared in the middle of Camp Nou and took the microphone; at 7.45 in the 'Auditorium 1899', Neymar answered the questions of the 122 journalists with official passes. Neymar, in broken Catalan and Portuguese, explained his happiness and joy to be able to stand there at that historic club and realise his dreams. He thanked God, explained that he had chosen to come to Barcelona not for money but to help the team win and to help Messi and the others be the best in the world, and to help Messi win lots more Ballons d'Or.

Young Neymar was polite, or rather he read the script that had been drummed into him – i.e. if you wanted to come to Barcelona and Camp Nou and win the sympathy of the people, the club and the fans, it was better to tread carefully, enter quietly and pay homage to the great players at the club and the undisputed genius that is Leo Messi. Neymar had been informed that his life at Barcelona would depend on how he got along with Messi. Ronaldinho, Eto'o, Ibrahimovic and David Villa had all had to pack their bags when it came to the crunch. Better to bow your head and not overshadow the champ. Neymar was humble and sometimes overdid it. So much so that some of the Brazilian journalists lost their rag and sniped, 'Fine that you will help Messi to be the best in the world and win Ballons d'Or but have you forgotten that there is a World Cup in a year's time?' Neymar moved away from praising the Barcelona fans and firmly answered, 'Helping Messi to be the best in the world has nothing to do with winning the World Cup. Just like all my teammates, we want to win.'

The polite young Neymar arrived at El Prat airport in Barcelona at 1.02pm, one hour and 45 minutes behind schedule, having boarded a private jet at the Antonio Carlos Jobim airport in Rio de Janeiro straight after playing for Brazil in a friendly against England. The Maracaná Stadium had been refurbished and updated for the World Cup and Neymar had received a nice surprise: the number 10 on his shirt. A symbolic number in football, it was the number Pelé wore for years and years. Felipão – Luiz Felipe Scolari – offered it to him; it was a gesture that showed the faith he has in Neymar. The young forward was to be the team's totem and leader.

Neymar played well in the first half. After ten minutes he had already taken three shots against Joe Hart, the England goalkeeper, but to no avail. In the second half, Neymar went off the boil. The fans continued to shout his name but his tricks failed to come off. The match ended 2–2 and Brazil's new number 10 missed out once again. He would get another chance.

The CBF gave their blessing and Neymar flew off to Catalunya to sign the contract and be introduced to the fans.

The Gulfstream G550 of Julio Iglesias (a devout Real Madrid fan), hired by Barcelona, hosted on board Neymar Pai, Neymar Jr's girlfriend Bruna Marquezine, his childhood friends Gil Cebolla, Gustavo, Gui Pita and Joclecio, who call themselves *parças* (short for *parceiros*: 'partners'). His staff were also there: Neymar's bodyguard Ismael, a huge black guy, and Eduardo Musa who manages Neymar's image.

Twelve hours later, the jet landed at Barcelona airport. Raúl Sanllehí was there to meet the Neymar party. Sanllehí was the man who had gone to Santos to finalise the deal for Neymar's signature. A minibus and two black vans took Neymar and his entourage to the Princesa Sofia Hotel, right next to Camp Nou. Nadine, his mother, and Rafaela, his sister, were waiting for him there. They had been in Barcelona for a week already, looking for a house.

Friends and family took a break. The *tour de force* for Neymar commenced. At 2.00pm, Neymar was smiling for the cameras next to the Barcelona crest, wearing his unmistakable cap on backwards and the white T-shirt of his sponsor, Nike.

Fifteen minutes later, Neymar walked into the Palau Blaugrana where he met his compatriot, Marcelinho Huertas, a player for Barça Regal, the basketball club. Then it was off to the hospital for the first part of his medical: radiography, echography and magnetic resonance.

At 3.29pm, more medical tests: this time at the Ciutat Esportiva de Sant Joan Despí. Neymar received the green light and was certified fit and able to play.

At 4.15 there was finally a break to get something to eat with his relatives and friends.

From Ciutat Esportiva he was taken to Camp Nou, where, at 6.05pm, he signed the contract tying him to Barcelona for five seasons. His salary would be €7 million a year with a further €2 million in performance bonuses (for games played and titles won). The break clause was set at €190 million.

Sandro Rosell, the chairman of FC Barcelona, signed first and then Neymar Jr and Neymar Pai followed. Every page was signed under the watchful eyes of the photographers and cameramen. Then the customary handshake between the chairman and the new star. Photos and more photos, with the vice-chairman and the director of sports, next to the Barcelona shirt.

At 6.20pm, the young Brazilian was in the changing rooms of Camp Nou to receive his kit. His locker would be next to two of his compatriots: Adriano and Dani Alves. The grand finale loomed ever closer.

It was 6.37pm when Neymar Jr walked along the tunnel and up the steps to one of the most famous pitches in the world.

The Camp Nou gates were meant to open to fans at 4.00pm but the 3,000 fans waiting outside made the gate-keeper open the gates fifteen minutes early. Slowly the stands began to fill up; the sunny and humid heat lingered in the air. The stands filled with people, banners and colours: so many young boys and girls from the city and the hinterland. So many Brazilians and South Americans. They had brought banners, flags, shirts, drinks and sandwiches to pass the time. There were tourists and foreigners who wanted to make the most of a special moment and had been to the Barcelona store to see the shirt (numberless) of Neymar Jr, next to that of Leo Messi (number 10).

On the big screen, the words *Benvingut Neymar Jr!* ('Welcome Neymar Jr!')

On the banners: 'Neymar da Silva: let's go and make history', '3,819 miles from New York to see you', 'Florentino [Perez, the Real Madrid chairman], you have no sea, nor Neymar', 'Neymar, we love you', etc. And flags galore: Catalan, Brazilian, as well as those of other South American countries …

But what was this Neymar like, the man whose appearance everyone was anticipating so eagerly? Sergi, sixteen, said, 'He is a star and Barcelona will prove that.' David, seventeen, said, 'He is good but let's see how he gets on here.' Natalia, sixteen, said, 'He is the best in the world.' Ivan, eleven, said, 'With Messi, they will form a partnership that has never been seen before. They will score 100 goals a season.' Carlos, eighteen, chimed in, 'If he gets on with Messi, he will be a success.' Camila, sixteen, said, 'He is an exceptional player and a bit of a hunk.' Lamin, fifteen, commented, 'I play with Santos on the Playstation because he played for them.'

Everyone had an opinion about the move. And when Pep Callau, the official spokesperson for Barcelona, started to walk round the stadium, few and far between were those who did not speak their mind. Some even burst into song and gave a rendition of the club's anthem. Brazilian music, images on the big screen to pass the time before the big moment. Three hundred and sixty children from FCB Escola, the club's football school, sat down on the pitch next to the light blue walkway which led to the centre of the pitch and the '*arc de triomphe*' that had been installed there. The orange sea of photographers and cameramen swayed from side to side on the lush green pitch. A good sign. The buzz of the crowd started to crescendo.

Neymar was here. He walked out on to the pitch, ball in one hand and waving with the other. The children's flags waved feverishly, the club's anthem boomed around the stadium, Rafaela and Bruna Marquezine took photo after photo from the bench and a tear of joy rolled down their cheeks. The 56,000-strong crowd roared a deafening cheer to welcome the new kid on the block.

Neymar had not beaten the record of 60,000 fans who came to see Ibrahimovic on 27 July 2009, nor the 80,000 fans who went to see Cristiano Ronaldo on 6 July 2009 at the

Santiago Bernabéu, but he doubled the 25,000 who came to
see Ronaldinho on 23 July 2003.

What did it feel like for a 21-year-old to arrive in another
country, another city, and be welcomed by 56,000 fans who
came just to see him, to watch him show off a few tricks and
hear him utter a few special words?

'It is something quite sensational, marvellous, hard to
believe. It was hard to fight back the tears,' is how Neymar
explained it later in an interview.

On the pitch, he was a complete professional. He was
up to the situation. That said, with his red and blue shirt
with no number on it, his new haircut with red highlights
but no Mohican, he looked tiny against the backdrop of the
immense stadium: a young kid who was rich and famous and
who, in front of hundreds of thousands of kids, does what
he likes doing: playing football. Under the arch, he pulled
a few tricks as the crowd went wild.

Laura Aparicio, Barça TV reporter, was responsible
for interviewing him. She asked him how he felt. '*Bona
tarda a tothom. Estic molt feliç per ser jugador del Barça i d'haver
aconseguit el meu somni.*' ('Good afternoon everyone. I am
so very happy to be a Barça player and to have achieved my
dream.')

Neymar was well prepared for the occasion and started in
Catalan. The fans showed their appreciation. At the end, he
signed off in Spanish: '*Muchas gracias y que Dios nos bendiga.
Visca el Barça.*' ('Many thanks, God bless you and long live
Barcelona.')

The perfect way to end the presentation in front of
56,000 fans. He did a lap of the pitch, booting balls up into
the stands; he waved and was overwhelmed with hugs from
the kids.

At 6.51pm, fourteen minutes after entering the pitch, he

was gone and heading for the changing rooms. The show was over.

A few at a time, the crowd slowly left the stadium, happy in the knowledge that Neymar was now with them: they had their new star.

Neymar's commitments were nowhere near over. In the Auditorium 1899, next to the Camp Nou stadium, the media were waiting patiently for the press conference. Next to Neymar was Andoni Zubizzareta, the sports director for the club and Joseph Maria Bartomeu, the vice-chairman of the club. The latter took the microphone and set the scene with the figures of the transfer: 'Neymar is costing us €57 million, more than we thought we were going to pay when we decided to contract him (€40 million). This was due to other clubs bargaining and pushing the price up.

'In addition, you should note that Neymar has come a year earlier than expected. The amount is split between these four businesses: DIS, TEISA, N&N and Santos. We have managed to get the deal done without intermediaries or agents, as always.'

More than that, Bartomeu was not willing to say. Due to a confidentiality clause in the agreement, he could not explain how the monies were split exactly. It put Neymar in second place, after Ibrahimovic, in the list of most expensive players the club had splashed out on. Bartomeu said that €10 million had already been paid whereas the rest would be paid over three years to the four companies which owned the rights to the player. The questions regarding the monies paid were fast and flowing from the journalists. The answer remained the same. The question would be discussed both in Spain and in Brazil for a long time. Those close to the deal claimed that the amount of the transfer was actually €70–75 million. €32 million was for Santos, without counting the earnings from the two friendly matches (one in the Camp Nou and the other in Brazil) and without counting the €8 million for the option rights to Victor Andrade, Gabriel and Giva, three kids playing for Peixe; €20 million was for N&N, Neymar Pai's company. The rest was to be split between DIS and Teisa.

Even these figures were not a dead cert, according to Florentino Pérez. The chairman of Real Madrid, a few days earlier, had claimed that he had withdrawn their offer for the Brazilian player because it would have cost the club a total of €150 million.

This bizarre conundrum was what eventually turned into 'Neymargate' a few months later, a controversy best described as a complete nightmare for the club from Catalunya.

On 5 December 2013, Jordi Cases, a Barcelona member, filed a complaint against Sandro Rosell, Barcelona's chairman, for 'wrongful misappropriation of funds by "diversion"' during the transfer process for the Brazilian star striker. Cases claimed that the overall amount paid by the club for Neymar was not the officially declared amount of €57 million but rather €94.4 million – €38 million more! Cases provided documentation allegedly showing that a portion of the total amount paid for Neymar was arranged through a series of 'contracts of financial engineering'. On 10 January 2014, the prosecutor for the *Audiencia Nacional* ('National Court') accepted the complaint and requested FIFA provide all the documentation relating to Neymar's agreement with N&N, as well as Santos's contracts with Neymar.

Three days later Barcelona asked not to be joined to the proceedings. So that was that …

On 22 January Pablo Ruz, the National Court judge, admitted Cases' complaint. The nine different contracts drawn up during the period running from November 2011 to September 2013 and which tied Neymar to Barcelona FC were investigated.

A day later, on 23 January 2014, Sandro Rosell, Barça's president, stood down from his post for good, stating that it was due to the 'unfair and reckless' behaviour complaint relating to the signing of the Brazilian golden boy. Joseph Maria Bartomeu, sporting vice-president, stepped up to the plate. He had the unenviable task of explaining the numbers behind the Neymar contracts. He admitted that the total cost of the transfer was €86.2 million and not €57.1 million, even though the latter was the declared figure. Barcelona, he said, had paid €40 million to N&N and €17.1 million to Santos for the transfer. The club had also signed a 'preferential option' side agreement with Santos over three players in the junior ranks. The value was €7.9 million plus a new contract with N&N for the day-to-day management of the young players. This N&N contract accounted for €400,000 per year over five years, amounting to a total of around €2 million. Totting up the figures, the total number came to €86.2 million, excluding bonuses. Barça would also be forking out a total of €56.7 million (i.e. €11.3 million per season) to their new number 11 in salary and signing-on fee. On 19 February 2014, the prosecution for the National Court requested that Barcelona be charged with tax fraud relating to Neymar's transfer. The alleged tax fraud was worth €9.1 million.

Leaving aside the controversy, let's get back to the press conference of 3 June 2013. Zubizzareta revealed the contents of Barcelona's first report about Neymar, which had been prepared by the club's technical team on 31 January 2011 after the Under-20 South American Championship final. He read out a few lines: '[Neymar] is one of the greatest talents in the world right now and if he continues to develop as he has done so far, he can become one of the greatest players in world football.'

Zubizzareta was also responsible for communicating the number on Neymar's shirt. 'Number 11 is Thiago's,' he said. 'We'll see.' (In the event, Thiago was to leave for Bayern Munich, so the number 11 was Neymar's.)

It was the turn of the child prodigy, wearing a Barça crested blue shirt with the collar up. Ney drew strength from his key words:

Heart: 'Madrid is a great club but I followed my heart
  and decided to come to Barcelona.'
Messi: 'I am one of the most fortunate men in the world
  to be able to play alongside Messi.'
Dream: 'I would like to thank Barcelona for helping me
  realise my childhood dream.'
Happiness: 'It is the most important thing. We did
  not follow the money. I do not believe I am worth
  €57 million.'
Joy: 'I will play my football. I hope to fit in straight away
  and to bring joy to the fans.'

The well-prepared answers carried on until 8.37pm when the press conference ended.

Before dinner, with his family and Sandro Rosell, there were a few more interviews to give to local media, Barça TV and TV3. Then the long day was over. Off to the hotel to get some rest.

The next day, the Gulfstream G550 would whisk Neymar off to Brasilia, followed by a helicopter ride to Goiânia, where Brazil were preparing for the Confederations Cup.

Chapter 28

Maracanã

The English writer, Alex Bellos, author of *Futebol: The Brazilian Way of Life*, claimed that the reference points for European history in the 20th century were the two World Wars; for the Brazilians, they were the World Cups.

In June 2013, it just so happened that the dress rehearsal for a World Cup became a 'war'. And for the first time in the country of *futebol*, for the first time in the history of the *jogo bonito* (the 'beautiful game'), football was in the firing line. Not the game, not the teams, not Brazil, but FIFA, the Brazilian government and the grandiose preparations for the 2014 World Cup.

The flame that lit the blue touchpaper was the increase in the public transport fares in São Paulo: a local issue that few would have expected to awaken the 'sleeping giant'. And yet, within a few days, there were demonstrations all over the country, spreading like wildfire due to social media. People were on the march in 80 cities; one million people were on the streets from Manaus to Rio de Janeiro, from São Paulo to Porto Alegre, something which had not happened for twenty years. Mainly peaceful processions were punctuated with sporadic outbursts of violence, ending up with a few getting hurt. The police reacted violently to the protests but there were policemen who, in front of the TV cameras, put down their weapons and joined the protesters in an act of solidarity. The crowds chanted, 'We are not here for the few hundred cents.'

In fact, even when the two largest cities withdrew the fare hikes for the buses, the underground and the trams, the protests did not stop. It was the people rising against the corruption which reigned supreme in the country; people showing their discontent with the schools, the hospitals, out-of-control public spending; people voicing their opinions about the government and the World Cup. It was the protest of a new middle class that Lula da Silva and Dilma Rousseff's governments helped create: a part of society that wanted to be in the first world but, seeing the constructions behind schedule, the failings, the hundreds of unresolved problems in Brazil, wanted to make its voice heard. It was a modern rebellion that had the country's young at its heart.

Before the onset of the protests, Carla Daudes, a 23-year-old Brazilian film director, posted a video online to explain why she was saying 'no' to the 2014 World Cup: 'It will cost $30 billion, more than the last three World Cups put together. Please tell me: do we need more stadiums in a country where illiteracy is at 21 per cent ... in a country listed at number 85 in the human development index, where 13 million people are starving and where many more die while waiting for treatment?'

Juca Kfouri from his office in São Paulo commented: 'The average attendance in the Brazilian stadiums is 15,000 spectators: less than the Soccer League [MLS] in the US, less than the Championship in England and the second division in Germany. Most of our stadiums were built during the dictatorship, when national integration was possible thanks to *futebol*. Well, we are doing the same with democracy. Instead of having a World Cup which is tailored to the needs of Brazil, those in power want to do as was done in South Africa and Germany. They have built and remodelled stadiums which, as we say in Brazil, are "white elephants", just like in

Manaus, in Brasilia and in Cuiabá. These are cities without a football team in the first or second divisions. It is absurd. Why spend all that money on stadiums and not a penny on the hospitals and schools?

'When Brazil was awarded the 2014 World Cup, the dissidents were few but now people are beginning to realise the truth and the Confederations Cup was the straw that broke the camel's back. People are now on the streets to make their opinions known.'

Brazilians had realised that the politicians were taking them for a ride and had used the World Cup to gain entry to the big league of world countries. It was a unique opportunity to show the world what Brazil was: a consolidated democracy, a leader in South America and a player in the big league. The World Cup was to be an incentive for more growth, more wealth, more well-being – it was to change the life of Brazilians, for the better. But it was not hard to see that the benefits of the World Cup would go to FIFA and into the hands of the select few while the average man was being kicked out of his home, out of the *favelas*, to make way for the stadiums, the training pitches, or indeed the sports complexes for the 2016 Olympics.

The deceit had been laid bare. There were rumours of swollen estimates like in the case of Maracana or Mané Garrincha in Brasilia; there was talk of bribes being given here and there, of buildings being promised but never built, of a clampdown on crime which turned out to be the calming of a few *favelas* by moving gangs from one side of the city to the other. It was becoming clear what the World Cup really was. The hundreds of banners and signs carried in the demonstrations around the cities of Brazil and pitched outside the stadiums shouted, 'Is the World Cup a priority for Brazil'; 'I want schools and hospitals not FIFA'; 'FIFA Go

Home'; 'The World Cup does not educate'; 'We do not want the World Cup, we want the metro'; 'No World Cup! Health and Education!'; 'When your child is ill, take him to the stadium?'; 'How many schools are there in Mané Garrincha?'; 'Japan: we exchange our football for their education'; 'Brazil, wake up: is one teacher worth more than one Neymar?'

In but a few days, seeing the protests on the streets of the Brazilian cities, the government did something that no one could have expected. The initial violent police enforcement action was replaced with an attitude of understanding and support for the uprising.

The fare hikes were withdrawn; Dilma announced investment in public transport; the *Supremo Tribunal Federal* (the highest court in Brazil) sentenced a corrupt senator to prison (albeit under house arrest), something which had never been seen before; the royalties from oil were invested in schools and education; it was announced that Congress would work even when Brazil were playing.

FIFA reacted by going underground. It removed its flags from the Copacabana Palace Hotel in Rio, operations HQ, and removed its logo from its official cars. Sepp Blatter, the chairman, who was irritated by the whistles he received at the opening ceremony of the Confederations Cup in Brasilia, stated, 'Football is more important here than the dissatisfaction of the people. The protesters are using football and the presence of the press as a platform to raise the profile of their protest.' He concluded by saying, 'Brazil asked for the World Cup. We did not force Brazil to host it. Brazil knew that to organise a good World Cup, they needed to build stadiums. So if the government has problems with its people, that's its problem, not ours.'

Marco Polo del Nero, vice-chairman of the Brazilian Football Federation and representative for Brazil at FIFA, stated that '199 million people are just focusing on working and there are only a few who are protesting.'

A rumour went round that if the disturbances carried on, FIFA could decide to play the last few matches of the tournament in another country. The flames were quickly doused on this rumour.

The government had a lot on its hands, what with the visit of Pope Francis at the end of July 2013. The atmosphere was tense but Brazil charged headstrong into the winds of angry protest.

Kfouri commented, 'It is curious, but when the country is doing well, the Brazilian team does not and there is no link with the fans. The demonstrations prove that the country is not doing well but Brazil [the team] is on form and the connection with the Brazilian people is renewed, reinforced. The national anthem is sung by the players, the fans and the protesters outside the stadiums with the same passion, the same voice.'

La Canarinha and the protest movement connected – unlike Pelé, who let slip an unfortunate comment ('Let's forget all this mess and think about Brazil') but immediately backtracked and withdrew it. Or unlike Ronaldo, 'O Fenómeno', who said, 'The World Cup is played in stadiums, not in hospitals.' He immediately withdrew the statement, saying that he was misinterpreted. These unfortunate comments aside, the Brazilian team was fully behind the protest. Dani Alves, Fred, Hulk and David Luiz were not afraid to make their opinions known when requested to do so by former players Romario and Rivaldo. Even Neymar got in on the action.

In the first match of the Confederations Cup, against Japan on 15 June, after three minutes, Neymar scored his first goal. Marcelo crossed the ball from the left. Fred controlled the ball with his chest and, with the ball still hanging in the air after the first bounce, Neymar let rip with an awesome strike that hit the back of the net at 98kmph after deflecting off the crossbar. The match, in the Mané Garrincha stadium, could not have got off to a better start.

Before the second match on 19 June 2013, the newly signed Barcelona striker posted on his Facebook page: 'Sad for all that is going on in Brazil. I had always hoped that it would not get to the point where people had to occupy the streets to obtain better conditions for transport, health, education and crime control. All of these are the DUTY of a government. My parents have worked hard to offer me and my sister a better quality of life … Today, thanks to the success I am honoured with, my comments could seem like populism but they are not. Let's lift the flag for the protesters all over Brazil. I am BRAZILIAN and I love my country!!! I have family and friends who live in Brazil. For this reason, I want Brazil to be a better, fairer, safer, healthier and more HONEST place!!! The only way I can represent and defend Brazil is by playing football. But as of this match, against Mexico, I will go on the pitch inspired by the movement of the people.'

Against Mexico in Fortaleza, the demonstrations and clashes reached the stadium. Inside, the fans were behind Brazil from the first to the last minute of the game. The signs and banners of protest were there but the fans and the team were on the same side. The national anthem was sung even when the music had stopped. Again it was Neymar who made the difference; in fact it was pretty much a one-man show. After nine minutes, a cross from Dani Alves, deflected by Rodriguez, was met by Neymar's punishing volley. Then in the 90th minute, he caught the Mexican defence off guard and delivered the ball on a plate to Jo, who made it two.

Mexico, Brazil's jinx, who had crucified La Canarinha in the 2012 Olympic final, were out. Neymar was man of the match for the second time.

The last Group A match was against Italy on Saturday 22 June in Salvador de Bahia. Five thousand protested against the spiralling costs of the World Cup. The banners told the story: 'We are in the streets for a better world'; 'We are not fighting the country but corruption'.

The demonstrators were held back by 1,500 policemen. During the match, they managed to get closer and tear gas was dispatched and rubber bullets were fired. As for the football, Brazil went into the match with a mixed track record against Italy. In March, in a friendly in Geneva, it had ended 2–2, and it was Brazil on the back foot that had had to claw back two goals in the second half.

This time Italy did not get a shot on goal in the first 45 minutes. The Brazilians dominated possession but did not achieve much. Brazil finally took the lead in first half stoppage time, the substitute Dante, wearing number 13, scoring the goal. Neymar's free kick was met by a header from Fred; Buffon parried but Dante put it in the back of the net.

The tables were turned in the second half. The *Azzurri* moved upfield and equalised with a beautiful goal from Giaccherini, who received the ball from a flick of the heel of Mario Balotelli. Neymar was not done yet though. When he was awarded a free kick on the edge of the area, the Italians put up a bit of resistance with the referee: they protested that Neymar had dived, that there was no foul, that Neymar was looking for the touch from Maggio.

Neymar got to the task in hand. A perfect shot and the ball left Buffon wrong-footed. A goal in the style of Zico or Didi. This was his third goal in three matches. Balotelli tried to replicate Neymar's goal from further back. He launched a missile but Julio Cesar blocked.

Brazil carried on. Fred scored to make it 3–1. Italy did not give up and pulled it back to 3–2. Maggio tried for the equaliser. But then Fred scored again to put the game beyond reach and the match ended 4–2.

The much anticipated duel between Balotelli and Neymar had ended with the first strike to 'Juninho'. Brazil had won, but it was not plain sailing. The European commentators were not convinced. John Carlin, British author and journalist, summed up in *El País* as follows: 'Those who have the image of Pelé, Rivelino, Tostão, or Zico and Sócrates, or even Romario as Brazilian football will not believe what their eyes have seen in the Confederations Cup, a trial run for next year's World Cup (but let's hope not). Brazil is reserved, defensive, without joy. There is no football samba. It is pure utilitarianism.'

His view was shared by many. Some talked of *antifutebol*, others hid their disappointment by focusing on the shining light that was Neymar.

In Brazil, they were critical but they were satisfied, as they knew that the Confederations Cup was a trial run for Scolari, the first step to putting together the World Cup team. Besides, they were in the semi-finals against Uruguay. The memories of Maracanazo on 16 July 1950 came flooding back.

Luis Suárez said he was aware of Ghiggia's goal at the front post; Edinson Cavani had only heard about it when he was twenty years old; Diego Forlán was philosophical: 'It is a clear reminder of what we are capable of but it does not help us today.'

Indeed the memories of the past do not help us face the present. It was true that Brazil did not burst on to the pitch with the same impact they had had in the other three matches but they controlled the game nonetheless. Julio Cesar and Neymar were there for Brazil. Cesar saved a penalty taken by Diego Forlán, his former Internazionale teammate. And that was it for Forlán, he did not pick himself up after missing the penalty.

Neymar did not score but he was central to the two Brazilian goals. A long ball from Paulinho right at the end of the first half found Neymar surrounded by Uruguayan defenders. He chested the ball down and had just enough time to boot it at Muslera who was off his line. Muslera parried but Fred was there in a flash and scrambled the ball in.

Five minutes from the end, it was Neymar again. He took a corner kick from the left; Paulinho jumped high and beat Cáceres and Muslera, who hesitated and was caught halfway: 2–1, and Brazil could now focus on who they would meet in the final.

It had not been a pretty match: patchy, dominated in the second half by the *Charrua* (Uruguay) who after Cavani's equaliser almost clinched victory. A football match with little football and a lot of tension and uncertainty, decided in the last few minutes of injury time. Brazil did not have the grace, the poetry, the *jogo bonito* which everyone expected. Brazil were focused on winning the game.

One memorable moment was provided by Neymar's kisses blown to Álvaro González. As the substituted Uruguayan midfielder exited the pitch he passed close to Neymar, who was about to take a corner, and insulted him. Neymar was mute and blew him a kiss. And another. To the pleasure of the crowd.

At Fortaleza, while the police were busy fighting back the protesters, Spain saw off Cesare Prandelli's Italy, beating them on penalties as they had in Euro 2008. After

120 minutes with no goals, the shoot-out finished 7–6 to the world champions.

La Roja (Spain) flew to Rio de Janeiro for the final everyone had been waiting for. Neymar spoke at the pre-match press conference and said, 'Now I can say it. It is the final everyone has been waiting for. Spain are the best in the world at the moment; they are the favourite, but Brazil has great players.'

Neymar said it was a great honour to be playing against his future teammates: 'It will be emotional. I wish them the best of luck – but not for this match.'

The press asked Neymar what the secret to beating Spain was: 'The important thing is not to be afraid. We must be brave enough to do our dribbling, try our tricks. Maracanã will be our twelfth man.'

Who, he was asked, did he fear the most in the Spanish team? 'Iker Casillas. He is in my FIFA team. He is the best goalkeeper in the world and one of the best of all time. I hope I can get one past him.' The press conference was over.

In the 44th minute of the final, Oscar, together with Neymar, went on a blistering counterattack. On the edge of the area, Oscar held the ball up. Neymar backtracked to stay onside and received the ball; he then released an Exocet missile, which slammed into the roof of the net with Casillas recoiling. It was a sensational goal and the number 10 celebrated by diving into the fans.

It was Neymar's fourth goal in the Confederations Cup, and it was a crucial one that put his team 2–0 up, Fred having scrambled a goal in after only one minute and 33 seconds. Neymar was there for that one as well, with a vital flick in the build-up. Fred sealed the game in second-half stoppage time for a final score of 3–0.

The Maracanã went into party mode. Spain, who had not lost an official game since the 2010 World Cup in South Africa (Switzerland 1 Spain 0) were done for. Brazil had put everything into the match and come out fighting: from David Luiz, who blocked a goal attempt from Pedro, to Neymar, who – apart from scoring – drew a foul that got Piqué sent off and forced Vicente del Bosque to replace full-back Arbeloa, who was not up to the challenge. The golden boy attacked and defended.

For his efforts he was named the best player of the tournament by FIFA. He had turned up to the Confederations Cup straight after signing for Barcelona with half the world watching how he would perform. It was not easy being put to the test in this way. But he had passed with flying colours.

In the heart of the Maracanã Stadium on the evening of 30 June 2013, the dream photo could be taken: Neymar biting the champions' medal behind the three trophies he so desired: the Confederations Cup, the Golden Ball for best player and the Bronze Boot for third best goalscorer.

Chapter 29
An Artist

A conversation with Vicente del Bosque

Vicente del Bosque, Spain's manager, walks up the stairs to the red building next to the main pitch. He chats with Toni Grande, his right-hand man, and then Julen Lopetegui, the Under-21s coach.

He has just come back from breakfast in the *Ciudad del Fútbol* cafeteria. In his office his day's work begins. At 10.30am, the base for the *Real Federación de Fútbol* in Las Rozas, 20km outside Madrid, is virtually deserted. There is just one youth team training on one of the adjacent pitches.

Del Bosque is relaxed. Spain are in the 2014 World Cup finals, having beaten Georgia on 15 October 2013 in Albacete. First in their group, Spain will take part in their fourteenth World Cup and will try to defend the trophy they won in South Africa in 2010. There are still lots of things to do in preparation for the Brazil World Cup but the main worry of getting three points to guarantee direct qualification is behind him. The polite and easygoing manager casts his mind back to the 2013 Confederations Cup final at Maracanã:

'Brazil were the better side and won the cup on merit. That's it. That simple. They were obviously favoured as they were playing on home turf and not only did they have the passion for football that is part of football in Brazil, the protests in the streets helped fire the spirit of the Brazilian team.

There is nothing unusual about the protests in a country where there are lots of social inequities. Top that off with the desire to beat the European and world champions and you have a motivated team. For them, it was a very important test. They wanted to do well, to shine in their home stadium, in front of their home crowd. Right from the national anthem, they were giants while we were small. Sure, there were moments where we were unlucky. To go down a goal in the first few minutes and then another just before half-time meant we could not really react. On a physical level, we arrived at the Maracanã after a hard semi-final against Italy and we only just got through, whereas they stormed through on a sea of joy. They had not suffered during the first stage of the competition. The semi-final was relatively straightforward and the final was not much of a challenge for them. I believe the atmosphere there helped them a lot. This is not an excuse. They played better than we did.'

Few expected to see a Brazil at that level before the match …
'I did. It is a compact team, well-structured and its great core strength is its ability to put our ball carriers under immense pressure. They also have great personalities. Neymar, without doubt, was one of the key players. He is a constant threat, playing on the left side.'

Did you know that beforehand?
'No. It was the first time we experienced Neymar.'

Did you read up on him? What advice did you give to your defenders? Or what advice did those from Barcelona, who had faced him in the Club World Cup, give you?
'I always have faith in Arbeloa who, on so many occasions, has sorted problems out for us on the wing, problems like

Neymar. Álvaro is a great player, an efficient marker but at Maracanã, there was nothing he could do. They were better than us. I assess a match from a collective point of view rather than individuals, I am talking about all of the players not just Arbeloa.'

Leaving that final to one side, what do you think about Neymar?
'I like him. He is one of those players who you do not see very often. He is heir to the Brazilian footballing tradition that was starting to fade. It is not that common nowadays to see a footballer who is able to take someone on on his own and dribble with flair and nimble footwork. He is an important player because when a team finds itself having to play against an overly defensive team, with too many players behind the ball, he can open things up and sort things out. Not just that he runs round players and scores goals, but that he creates risky situations for the other team or gets free kicks near the area.

'Neymar represents this type of player. He strikes the ball beautifully, he is ambidextrous, he is a *goleador*, always in the right place, open on the left side; he is able to get out of tricky situations on that side. I am not saying he cannot play in another position but that is his best position. Just like Messi, who started on the wings and then moved to a fake number 9 position. This is the job of the manager: all players can play in different positions, but all players have their ideal position.'

Seeing as you mentioned him, let's compare Messi and Neymar.
'For the time being, it is too soon to be making comparisons, seeing as Neymar has just arrived at Barcelona. Neymar is known for what he did at Santos and in the Confederations Cup, which is his major reference point.

'Messi is extraordinary. He has been at the top of the footballing best player tables for the last few years. Since starting at Barcelona almost ten years ago, he has been consistent and progressive. Every year he has achieved more awards, more records and new titles.

'Messi and Neymar are very ambitious. They are able to turn a match around but both need a well organised team behind them to be the best and to release their full potential. In that sense, they are quite similar. We will need time to get to know Neymar, to understand if he can adapt to Barcelona and whether he wants to be joint front runner with Messi or try and make history. Messi and Cristiano Ronaldo have done it and I believe they are a good example for world football.'

And what do you think about Cristiano Ronaldo and Neymar?
'Cristiano is all power, speed, left-footed and right-footed shots, headers, penalties, free kicks. He is an "animal". He is less creative than Neymar and Messi and is less confident in close-quarter dribbling. He needs room to play. He does not have the repertoire of Neymar, who is lighter, but is still awe-inspiring. At Manchester United, Ronaldo gained a huge amount of experience and, since joining Madrid, he has always played at the highest level. Neymar is a football artist and Spanish football needs players like this.'

How long will Neymar take to adapt?
'You never can tell how long it will take a player to adapt. Argentinian players, for example, adapt a lot more easily and quickly to our style of football and to our league. Almost none of the Argentinian players who have come to play in Europe have failed and they have produced what was expected of them. They are the Germans of South America. They have work ethic and character. Whereas the Brazilians

are a mixed bag. Some have triumphed but others have struggled to adapt. That's why I think we need to wait and be patient with Neymar. He is at a club that can help him resolve lots of issues. If he is clever and smart and he keeps his eyes open, he will fit in quickly. He has arrived here with the reputation of a star but he has shown already that he has a positive and collaborative attitude. Earning the team's sympathies and support as he has done, with his humble nature, is very positive. He understood right from the start that he has been placed in a team where there are clear leaders. The player who gets a place in this special team has to win the trust of the rest of the team and the veterans. And Neymar came on merit. His personality will tell us about what Neymar can do in Europe. His quality and talent are boundless but even Robinho had buckets full of talent, and he was not a huge success at Madrid.

'If Neymar shows he has character and is a professional he will progress and have a long career at Barcelona. Just like Ronaldinho, who played a key role in the modern era of Barcelona. When he arrived, the team were in the doldrums and he lifted them up and turned the team's mentality around in but a few years. Then Messi came along and overtook him.'

How do you see Neymar and Messi in the World Cup? The dream of both is to win it.
'Whether they like it or not, they are better the better the team is. If Brazil win, Neymar will come off stronger and Messi will be downbeaten, and if Argentina win, the opposite – even though I don't think these two players need to win the World Cup to confirm their status. They are players who, when the rest of the team are out of ideas, get the ball and do something magical. They are special players.'

What are the chances for Brazil and Argentina?
'Argentina are playing very well; they have a good chance of winning. They have international players and Messi. The Brazilians are the favourites, however. [Because of] the setting and because they have an aggressive squad, which is compact with flashes of brilliance. From the midfield to the wings, they are very strong. They have Dani Alves and Marcelo, who are unique. Two centre forwards who are solid and a well-equipped centre midfield ... With two "animals" like Hulk and Fred up front and Neymar, who is the perfect counterbalance.'

Chapter 30

A good kid

A conversation with Luiz Felipe Scolari,
aka Felipão

It does not matter where he is, Felipão never misses out on his morning walk. He leaves the hotel early in the morning in his tracksuit, with his closest assistants, Carlo Alberto Parreira and Flávio Teixeira, 'O Murtosa', even though the local police advise against it as they had in Colombia.

It is a good way to keep fit and to clear your head before a match. It is only a friendly but it is still important as, after the Confederations Cup and before the World Cup, this is the only way to prepare.

In a large Swiss hotel, 65-year-old Luiz Felipe Scolari, the man who was rushed in to replace Mano Menezes in November 2012 to put Brazil back on track, talks about his future. He collapses in a large armchair, tired after his morning walk. He reflects on the 2014 World Cup and on Brazil. He is the manager who won the fifth and last World Cup for Brazil in 2002. He is the coach who every single Brazilian is hoping will win the World Cup on home soil. The bookies have lowered the odds on Brazil winning following the Confederations Cup victory (which was Brazil's third successive Confederations Cup win, their fourth overall). Scolari wants to keep people's feet on the ground, however.

'Our performance in the Confederations Cup was good

and we played well in the final against Spain. We cannot say that Brazil is the best team in the world at the moment. We are not a step ahead of the rest as we were 20 or 30 years ago. This is not the Brazil of 1970. Today, it is much more of a level playing field. Let's say that the win against Spain has given us a boost of confidence and confirmed that we are on the right track.

'We have tried to build a team that is well organised from a tactical point of view; since the World Cup in 2006, the renewal has been a lengthy process, as after that World Cup seven or eight players left the national team. We put together a group of players who enjoy playing for their country and play with their heart. We want a team able to face up to the best in the world in the 2014 World Cup. In the World Cup, there will be South American and European teams with great players and good structures.

'There's Spain, which has a similar style to Barcelona. Germany is a great team which knows how to renew itself by putting creative and talented young players in. Argentina is not just Leo Messi. Italy is a nation different from the stereotypes of the past: different to the tradition of a team able only to defend and mark the opposition.

'We will have the advantage of playing at home in front of our fans and this will give us an edge but we are not superior to other teams like Argentina, Germany or Spain.'

OK. But will you, Mr Scolari, be able to make the Brazilians forget about O Maracanaço [the 1950 World Cup final defeat] ?
'In Brazil, we look at lots of things via statistics: Italy played two World Cups in Italy. It won one and lost one. Germany has played two at home: it won one and lost one. We have only played one and we lost it. Now we want to not prove the statistics wrong.'

It is a good answer. There's no doubt about it, Scolari is cunning and ironic; he moves on from the World Cup to talk about Neymar, the star of the moment.

When did you get to know him?
'Four or five years ago, when he was starting to become famous at Santos, when he played his first matches during Vágner Mancini's reign.'

What do you think about him?
'He is a very good player and very professional. Yes, he is a master of the ball. Just like Cristiano Ronaldo [Scolari, as coach for Portugal from 2002 to 2008, got to know Cristiano well]. He is always ready to train, to push things to the limit, to work hard and improve himself. Neymar wants to learn; he wants to evolve technically and not hold back even when he is asked to go in defence. For a creative player like him, running back and marking a player on the other team is difficult for him but he does it and he does it well. Neymar is always ready to try something new and add it to his repertoire.'

A repertoire full of magical tricks. Which is your favourite?
'His best qualities are his incredible dribbling, his improvisation and his imagination. They are natural gifts that he was born with. What we can teach him is the tactics that help develop his skills. It is what Muricy [Ramalho] did at Santos, what we did in the national team and what Tata Martino is doing at Barcelona: to make Neymar understand that he needs to play for the team and that he has to use his individual skills for the team. This is the spirit we want from him. It is something you learn bit by bit. It is life that teaches you, the coaches who advise you and the games, championships and tournaments that give you the experience you need.

This is the evolution Messi went through at Barcelona and it appears to be the evolution Neymar is going through as well.'

How is Neymar doing at Barcelona, in your opinion?
'Well, very well. He is adapting very quickly, he has a good relationship with Messi and he is playing more for the team than for himself. This will be useful for Brazil.'

What can Spanish and European football give him?
'I am convinced that Neymar will learn a lot tactically and strategically. These are two things that are fundamental in Europe. In Brazil, the style is different. Football has a different feel, improvisation is more prevalent. Then there is the workload and the number of matches in a season. And let's not forget the climate. In Brazil, when it's really cold in Santos it's 10–15°C. In Europe, games are played when it's five degrees below zero, when it's snowing – something which Neymar will need to adapt to.'

Neymar, Messi and Cristiano Ronaldo are all in the same league. What's your view?
'They have different features. Neymar is more like Messi than Cristiano. Neymar plays short, in small spaces and gets out of tight spots when surrounded by players. Messi is similar: in five metres he can skip past two defenders. Cristiano needs space to use his power. But in all three cases, there is no doubt: these are the best three strikers in the world – even if Neymar is a hybrid: he is a 9, an 11, an 8, a 7 and a 10. I am certain that in the next few years he will be a world icon, a status that he will easily achieve playing in La Liga as European football is better structured than Brazilian from this perspective. Eastern Europe, the Middle East and all of Asia watch the European leagues and Champions League.

Not many people watch the Brazilian leagues apart from some key matches.'

But Neymar is already an idol. Some have even called him the new Pelé – an inheritance and a responsibility that could weigh him down ...
'Neymar is a well-balanced person. He is strong, mentally. He does not let the things people say about him affect him. Neymar is on his own path.'

Leaving football aside for a minute, what are the aspects of his personality that have led to him becoming a media phenomenon?
'He is a good kid. He is a good son. I have seen him at lots of sporting events and he has an attitude towards his father that few have in public. He is affectionate, funny, simple and within the team his behaviour is spectacular, both in front of the veterans and the new arrivals. He is extrovert, funny and always joking. He is a party animal and always has a new look. I always take the mickey out of his hairstyles. I say to him, "Very nice. You look good with a yellow Mohican." It is something of a running joke between us.'

Have you ever told him to cut it off?
'No. I limit myself to joking about it.'

No advice about hairstyles? Surely you must have given him some advice.
'Yes. When we speak, I advise him to look after his body, day by day, because this is what his bread and butter is as a footballer. He needs to be in tip-top shape to do what he does on the pitch. I tell him to manage his fame appropriately and his earnings, to be careful about his life off the pitch, about who he mixes with, as they can take you down the wrong path. Above all I tell him to never stop growing and trying to be the best that he can be.'

Chapter 31

Barcelona

It was gala evening at the Grand Connaught Rooms in London. Dinner jackets, bow ties, fine dining, speeches and toasts. It was a birthday party. Football was celebrating its 150th anniversary. On this site, in Great Queen Street in the heart of London, the Freemason's Tavern used to stand. It was there that, on 26 October 1883, Sir Ebenezer Cobb Morley, founder and captain of Barnes Football Club, and representatives of eleven other clubs and sporting associations, met 'with the aim of promoting a code of common rules and more generally to adopt articles of association', as it was reported in the *London Daily News*. It was there that, amid several debates, modern football and the first national football federation was born: the Football Association.

The party at the Grand Connaught was hosted by none other than Prince William, chairman of the FA and a keen Aston Villa fan. In his speech, he pointed out that 'football is a great force in the world and can do a great deal of good. There are a lot of people who love it, respect it and enjoy football like nothing else in their life'. At the end, he offered a toast to the guests and to the next 150 years of the FA and football.

A few hours earlier, 1,488km away, another football party was being celebrated: Barcelona *vs.* Real Madrid. It was *El Clásico* number 225, and the first for Neymar Jr in the Barça shirt.

'It is the match in which every footballer hopes to play, to show their best *futebol*,' explained Neymar to Barça TV. He thought back to other classic matches. The *clásico* he recalled the best was when Ronaldinho, in the Santiago Bernabéu, scored two goals and received a standing ovation from the Madrid fans, on 19 November 2005. Neymar said he had experienced lots of good 'classic' matches in Brazil. The first he played was against Palmeiras, a semi-final, which Santos won; then the final of the Paulistão, which Santos lost to Corinthians; and then against São Paulo. Neymar continued, 'There is the rivalry during the week leading up to the match, just like here. The only thing everyone is talking about is the match; it is the most-talked about topic in the newspapers and by the fans. Even the players who are friends with the players on the other team have a few digs and jibes with their friends on the opposing team. That is the beautiful thing about football.'

He was aware that, for him, the *clásico* on Saturday, 26 October 2013 was extremely important. He was hoping to play well and win.

Almost three months had gone by since Neymar joined Barcelona. After the Confederations Cup, Neymar underwent a tonsillectomy and an operation to correct his nasal septum. Then a short break with friends. Bruna, his girlfriend, had finished *Dancing with the Stars* in Brazil and they joined up with her friends in Europe: Rome and Athens. Monuments and ancient history for her; sun, sea, beaches, relaxation and parties for Neymar. Just what the doctor ordered, before catching the flight back to Ciudad Condal.

He arrived in Barcelona on the morning of 28 July. The next day he would meet his new teammates. A medical would be followed by his first training session in the *Ciutat Esportiva* with Messi & Co. At the end of the session, Neymar tweeted, '*meu sonho virou realidade. Obrigado Senhor!*' ('My dreams have come true. Thank you Lord!')

On 30 July he was already on a plane to Poland for a friendly against Lechia Gdansk. In the PGE Arena, the Polish fans stuck up a banner which was a bit dated (it showed images of Guardiola, Messi, Puyol and Cruyff with the slogan in Catalan *Tots units fem força* ('Together we are stronger'). They wanted to see Messi and Neymar on the pitch. They were disappointed for the sake of a few minutes. Neymar started on the bench and came on in the 78th minute, taking the place of Alexis, but Messi had already been substituted. So Neymar's debut for Barcelona consisted of twelve minutes in a match that ended up a 2–2 draw. Not much, granted, but for Neymar it was enough to put a smile on his face: 'Barcelona is much better than I thought. It is a great feeling. I am very happy to be able to speak to Messi, to be near Xavi and Iniesta.' He said he was working to adapt as quickly as possible to Barça's style of play, '*el más bonito del mondo*' ('the best in the world').

He could not wait to play his first match in Camp Nou.

On 2 August, Neymar got his chance in the 'Trofeo Joan Gamper', a special match. Barcelona were playing Santos, Neymar's old club.

The slogan for the tournament read *Nueva temporada, nuevos sueños* ('New season, new dreams'). All true. Barça had a new coach: Gerardo 'El Tata' Martino, the Argentinian who had played for Newell's Old Boys in Rosario, the city where Leo Messi was born and started playing football. The replacement had been organised quickly after Tito Vilanova had had to resign due to bad health, cancer of the parotid gland. Barça also had a new star: Neymar was making his debut, together with Tata. And Barcelona had just said farewell to Antoni Ramallets, who had died aged 89. The 'Cat of

Maracanã' was one of the historic players of the club, winner of five cups as Barça goalkeeper.

In the heat of an August evening, 81,000 fans filled the Camp Nou stadium and wanted to pay homage to the number 1 who had passed away and to understand what they could expect from the year ahead.

The fans were to go home happy and safe in the knowledge that the future would be a bright one. Barcelona absolutely obliterated Santos 8–0. Leo Messi opened the scoring and in half an hour the game was over. Neymar came on in the second half, after an incident where a pitch invader wanted to hug him: eight security guards were needed to hold the man down. Neymar had the number 11 on his back and received a standing ovation from the crowd.

Neymar played on the left side, where he was marked by Arouca. He was on the pitch with Messi for fifteen minutes. He showed off a few tricks but seemed more interested in passing the ball around rather than going for goal. He avoided going over the top but he nonetheless provided the perfect assist for the sixth goal, scored by Cesc Fàbregas. Towards the end, in the deluge of goals, he got the chance to score but pinged Vladimir's crossbar.

Neymar's post-match comment was, 'It is a strange sensation. I am happy for the win for my team and my new teammates but sad for my teammates at Santos who I care about.'

The Brazilian papers were hard on Peixe the next day. *Lance* wrote, 'What a disgrace! Without even trying and with Neymar on the pitch in the second half only, Barça humiliates Santos.' The paper coined a phrase for the best duo in the world, the neology 'LioNey': a catchy expression that has slowly gained ground with the press.

After the 'Gamper' came the 'Peace Tour': the Barcelona team headed off to a clinic in Bloomfield Stadium in Tel Aviv with Israeli and Palestinian children. Thereafter they would begin their Asian tour, which would take them to Thailand and Malaysia.

Santos, on the other hand, headed home with their tails between their legs. It was a crisis and fans held demonstrations before the *clásico* between Santos and Corinthians.

After the team's training session at the CT Rei Pelé and before the press conference (where Edu Dracena, the captain, and Odilio Rodrigues Filho, the vice-chairman, tried to reassure the press), O Rei and Victor Andrade shared their thoughts about Neymar playing at Camp Nou. Victor, who was three years younger than Neymar and came through the youth teams at Santos, had learned a lot from his ex-colleague: 'When I made the first team, he helped me, he gave me good advice on how to behave on the pitch. He told me not to be nervous; he taught me when is the right moment to dribble and when it is better to pass the ball. Do this, do that, hold that position, stay unmarked. I have followed his advice and thank God everything is going well.'

The young kid for Santos explained, 'On the pitch, Neymar was spectacular, quick, agile and improvised all the time. He did what no one expected. He was surely one of the best players I had ever seen and a true teammate. Off the pitch, he was different. He was funny and liked being with his friends and family. I have to say that I had a great time with him.'

Talking about Neymar playing for Barcelona, Victor said, 'It was weird having him as an opponent, especially as three months ago he was playing next to me. It was not a problem as when the referee blows the whistle, you do not think too much about it.'

He continued by saying that they did not talk much about

football but more about Neymar feeling homesick: 'It is hard living far away from Brazil.'

What was worrying Ricardo Rosa, physical trainer for Santos, was not Neymar's homesickness but his weight. He saw that the Barcelona staff wanted Neymar to put on three kilos to adapt to European football and he was very concerned: 'It could be a disaster. He could lose his qualities as has happened to other players. Sure, if you look at Neymar, you see he is thin and has no muscles but he is very, very strong. His legs are made for running, for dribbling and for skipping around other players. He is agile, quick and, unlike other strikers, he has incredible stamina. He never gets tired and can repeat moves, one, two, three, four, five times.

'He takes knocks from defenders. Sure, he goes down but he does not get seriously hurt. It would be a shame if they made him put on bulk and muscles.'

Weight was not the only thing causing issues between Spain and Brazil. There was also Neymar's anaemia. The Spanish press spread a rumour that he was on a diet and taking vitamin supplements to deal with a low level of iron in his blood. Luiz Felipe Scolari lost his patience: 'It's as though they [Barcelona] know everything and we are the third world and we do not know anything. After an operation it is normal that he has lost weight but he will gain it back with time. When he eats like a horse at midday, at three in the afternoon and six and nine, he is great. He is on form. If it wasn't like this, he would not play as he is doing for Barcelona.'

Felipão was not wrong, as, during the Asian tour, Neymar was on form.

On 7 August, in the friendly against Thailand in the Rajamangala national stadium in Bangkok, he scored his first goal. In the 11th minute, Messi was on the edge of the area and fed the ball out to the left for Fàbregas, who whipped the ball in. Neymar stuck his foot out and put the ball in the back of the net. The celebration – a quick hug with his teammates – was reserved compared to those he was used to performing in Brazil.

It was different when it came to his first goal that really counted. On 21 August, Barcelona were playing in the first leg of the Spanish Super Cup at the Vicente Calderón. Four days earlier, Neymar had played his first *Liga* match, against Levante. He came on to replace Messi in the 63rd minute (Tata Martino is a fan of mixing things up and rotating players), when the game was already won: 6–0 to Barça.

In the Calderón, David Villa, formerly of Barcelona, now playing for Atlético Madrid, pulled off a fantastic volley: 1–0 to the Red-and-Whites. Messi had to go off at half-time with a muscle problem. It seemed as though Atlético were going to have an easy ride. Alexis and Mascherano were the only Barça players holding the fort. Neymar came on in the 59th minute, replacing Pedro. Seven minutes later, he put Barcelona back on level terms. Xavi passed to Dani Alves on the right; the Brazilian crossed to the back post; Juanfran did not realise Neymar was arriving behind him. The number 11 beat Juanfran to the ball and headed in. Courtois could not get there. It was Neymar's first official goal. He hugged Alves and the others and headed over to the bench to Tata and his teammates. It was a goal that earned Neymar his first trophy with Barcelona. The return leg in Camp Nou finished 0–0 and the cup was Barça's.

Eight matches later came Neymar's first goal in *La Liga*. It was against Real Sociedad on 24 September. It was not a pretty goal: it was the result of mistakes by the other side's defence. Claudio Bravo, the goalkeeper, and Liassine Cadamoro, the central defender, turned an innocent-looking cross from Alexis into a scuffle over the line for the *Blaugrana* number 11. Neymar confessed after the match: 'The ball crossed the line crying.' He dedicated the goal to his son, David Lucca. Before the match, he had introduced David to the fans, just as Leo Messi had with Thiago, his firstborn.

Two other Brazilian ex-Barça players had got their goal-scoring tally off to a start against Real Sociedad: Romario in 1993 and Rivaldo in 1997. A simple coincidence, but Neymar was following in the footsteps of the great Brazilian players who had mesmerised Camp Nou and made history with Barcelona FC. First among these was Evaristo de Macedo: he came from Club de Regatas Flamengo and from 1958 to 1961 he scored 178 goals in 226 matches. Then came Romário Faria da Souza, better known as Romario. He joined from PSV Eindhoven and from 1993 until halfway through the 1994/95 season he played for the Dream Team. Everyone remembers the three goals he scored in a *clásico* against Real Madrid. Then came Giovanni, a star from Santos, then Ronaldo Luís Nazário da Lima, 'O Fenómeno', then Sonny Anderson, then Rivaldo and finally the smiler, Ronaldinho.

Neymar is the latest in a long tradition of great Brazilian players and he was carving out his place and adapting to the Barça style of play.

He had been scoring fewer goals compared to his Santos days but against Real Madrid he made his fifth assist to Messi. He had already played in the Champions League, against Ajax on 18 September. At only 21, he had already played 300 professional games.

On 1 October 2013, against Celtic, Neymar showed his maturity. On the historic pitch where football has been played since 1888, when Brother Walfrid, Andrew Kerins founded the four-leaf clover club in order to drum up funds for charity, Neymar was at the helm, as Messi was not playing.

The number 11 was incisive, decisive, brave and defence-breaking. He started with the short game, he dribbled but without overdoing it, he led the attack but helped out in defence as well. Lustig got a yellow card thanks to Neymar and Brown a red after having kicked him in the back. Two fantastic saves from Fraser Forster prevented Neymar from getting his goal in 'Paradise' (as described on one of the Celtic banners in the crowd) but he set up the counterattack that allowed Fàbregas to score.

The match earned him the praise of Tata Martino and his teammates but criticism from Neil Lennon. The Celtic manager accused him of being too theatrical: 'This is a physical game. Neymar does not help anyone by overegging it when he is fouled.'

Here we were again. The story of the player who goes down at the slightest touch. A controversy which got everyone involved, including José Mourinho and Tata Martino. One weighed in against the 'diver'; the other argued that referees did not blow the whistle when Neymar was fouled.

Leaving the controversy to one side, by the eve of *El Clásico*, 'Juninho' was feeling positive. He had played three matches in the Champions League, including one against Milan at San Siro, where he was up against his friend Robinho, two Spanish Super Cup matches and nine in *La Liga*. He had scored a hat-trick in a match against Valladolid. Above all, he had shown that, against all odds, he had been able to adapt to European football very quickly. He had been able to stand in for Messi when the Argentinian was not playing and to support the number 10 when he was not firing on all cylinders. Neymar had made friends in the dressing room and the fans loved him (sooner than expected). His life at Barcelona was going great guns in all respects.

He has showed none of the excesses that other Brazilians

have been famous for. He lives in the city in a nice part of Ciudad Condal in a rented house over three floors near to Avenida Pearson. He is far away from Castelldefels where Ronaldinho and Ronaldo lived and where Messi lives. Neymar Pai lives with his son and keeps a close eye on Neymar Jr. Nadine and Neymar's sister Rafaela are in Santos but travel to Barcelona once a month with the 'Toiss', Neymar's best friends. Bruna is in Brazil due to work commitments.

Neymar does not go out much. He goes for a meal or two, mainly to Japanese restaurants like Ikibana, il Nomo and lo Shunka. He often goes with Álvaro Costa, son of Pep, the service manager for Neymar at Barcelona; sometimes with Dani Alves and Adriano, his best friends in the team. It was Dani who helped him find a hairdresser worthy of the task, at Esplugues de Llobregat. When he is not training or playing, Neymar spends a lot of time at home. Brazilian music, videos, takeaways and PlayStation occupy his time: FIFA, Grand Theft Auto and Call of Duty are his favourite videogames. He follows Santos on the TV but is not too interested in following *La Liga* or the Champions League.

The day of *El Clásico* finally arrived. It was 26 October 2013. All the big guns were out: Messi, Cristiano Ronaldo and Gareth Bale, the Welshman who signed for €91 or €101 million, depending on who you speak to, and, of course, Neymar. It was a *clásico* missing certain protagonists: José Mourinho, who had turned the match into a psychological battle as much as anything else, Tito Vilanova, who was poked in the eye, and Pep Guardiola, the footballing philosopher, who was by then plying his trade in Germany.

The list of *El Clásico* debutants on the day was long: Neymar, Bale, Carlo Ancelotti and Zinedine Zidane (the Frenchman had seen many a Real Madrid–Barcelona contest, of course, but never from the bench as assistant manager) and last but not least Tata Martino. *La Liga* had been closely fought at the top of the table and, at this point of the season, Barcelona were just nudging ahead of Real by three points.

Ancelotti goaded, 'Everyone thinks Barça is the favourite and that is fine by us.' Martino's riposte was 'Who is the favourite will be shown during the 90 minutes of the game.'

At eight in the evening, when the guests at football's 150th anniversary were starting dinner in London, the result of the match was already known. Camp Nou was on its feet when Neymar Jr exited the pitch. He had scored and provided an assist. Just like Romario, Eto'o, Villa and Ibrahimovic, Neymar had been a key player in Barcelona's win.

Iniesta on the edge of the area had given the ball to Neymar on the left. The Number 11 had fired the ball hard along the ground and it went straight between the legs of Caravajal, his marker, and Varane who had deflected the ball ever so slightly and put Diego Lopez out of sync. Goal! It was Neymar's first goal in the *clásico* and it put Barça ahead. Neymar continued to impress, providing, on the counterattack, an assist for Alexis, the *Niño Maravilla*, who with a stunning shot signed, sealed and delivered victory to Barcelona.

As is the tradition after a *clásico*, there were the usual squabbles and controversy: the inconsistent officiating by referee Undiano (he failed to give a penalty for a foul by Mascherano on Cristiano Ronaldo); the weak line-up sent out by Ancelotti (the newspapers accused him of gifting the first half to Barcelona). But in the deluge of photographs and news stories, the world press had no doubts that a star was born: Neymar shone, and shone bright. The kid from Mogi das Cruzes had made the news and filled the column inches. His photo was everywhere in the sporting press.

The best photo was the one on the front page of

La Vanguardia: Neymar, with his back to the camera, bearing the number 11 to the world and celebrating his goal in front of the stands, arms open like Christ the Redeemer in Rio de Janeiro. The headline that captured the moment perfectly came from *L'Equipe*: 'Neymar the Prince of Camp Nou'.

There is nothing more to say.

A career in numbers

Name: Neymar da Silva Santos Junior
Nickname: Juninho, Ney
Date of birth: 5 February 1992
Place of birth: Mogi das Cruzes, São Paulo, Brazil
Nationality: Brazilian
Parents: Neymar da Silva Santos and Nadine Gonçalves
Sister: Rafaela
Son: David Lucca
Height: 1.74m
Weight: 64.5kg
Position: Forward
Number: 11 (Santos, Barcelona); 10 (Brazil)

Teams:
Clube de Regatas Tumiaru
Gremetal
Portuguesa Santista
Santos (2004–2013)
Barcelona (2013–)

Santos
First appearance for first team: 7 March 2009
against Oeste of Itápolis
First goal: 15 March 2009 against Mogi Mirim

Competition appearances and goals:

Paulista league and Brazilian league:	179	107
Brazil Cup:	15	13
Continental Cups:	29	15
Other trophies:	7	3

Barcelona

First appearance: 30 July 2013 against Lechia Gdansk
First goal: 7 August 2013 against Thailand
First goal in an official match: 21 August 2013 against Atlético
Madrid (Spanish Super Cup)

Competition appearances and goals (up to 25 February 2014)

La Liga:	18	7
Super Cup:	2	1
Copa del Rey:	4	2
Europe:	7	3

Brazil

First appearance: 10 August 2010, against USA
(friendly match)
First goal: 10 August 2010, against USA (friendly match)

Appearances and goals (up to 25 February 2014)

63   41

Tournaments:

Under-17 World Cup, 2009
Under-20 South American Cup, 2011
Copa America 2011
Superclásico de las Americas 2011, 2012
Olympics, 2012
Confederations Cup, 2013

Titles won
Santos
Paulista League, 2010, 2011, 2012
Brazil Cup 2010
Copa Libertadores 2011
Recopa Sudamericana 2012

Barcelona
Spanish Supercup, 2013

Brazil
Under-20 South American Cup, 2011
Superclásico de las Americas, 2011, 2012
Olympic silver medal, 2012
Confederations Cup, 2013

Individual awards
Best player in the Paulista league, 2010, 2011, 2012
Best player in the Brazilian league, 2011
Best young player in the world (*World Soccer* award), 2011
South American player of the year, 2011, 2012
Bota de ouro ('Golden Boot' – *Placar*/ESPN Brazil award),
2010, 2011, 2012
FIFA Puskás Award (best goal of the year), 2011
Confederations Cup 'Ballon d'Or'
(player of the tournament), 2013

Bibliography

Books

Annuario del calcio mondiale, Bologna, Cantelli, 1988

Assaf, R. & Martins, C., *Campeonato carioca: 96 anos de história 1902–1997*, Rio de Janeiro, Irradiação Cultural, 1997

Bellos, A., *Futebol: The Brazilian Way of Life*, London, Bloomsbury Publishing, 2012

Bioy Casares, A., *Unos días en Brasil (Diario de viaje)* Madrid, La Compañia de los Libros, 2010

Bouchard, J.-Ph. & Constant, A., *Un siècle de football*, Paris, Calmann-Levy, 2005

Burgarelli, R., *Neymar de A a Z*, São Paulo, Panda Books, 2013

Casagrande Jr., W. & Ribeiro, G., *Casagrande e seus demonios*, Rio de Janeiro, Globo Livros, 2013

Castro, R., *Estrela solitária Um brasileiro chamado Garrincha*, São Paulo, Companhia Das Letras, 1995

Cocco, G., *Mundo Braz*, Rio de Janeiro, Record, 2009

Franco Júnior, H., *A dança dos deuses: Futebol, Sociedade Cultura*, São Paulo, Companhia das Letras, 2007

García-Ochoa, J.I., *Neymar: El nuevo O' Rei*, Madrid, Al Poste, 2013

Jatene, C., *10 décadas: a História do Santos Futebol Clube*, São Paulo, Companhia Editora Nacional, 2012

Kfouri, J., *Por que não desisto – Futebol, Poder e Política*, São Paulo, Disal Editora, 2009

Mills, J., *Charles Miller: O Pai do futebol brasileiro*, São Paulo, Panda Books, 2011,

Moré, I. & Betting, M., *Neymar – Conversa entre pai e filho*, São Paulo, Universo dos Libros, 2013

Napoleão, A.C. & Assaf, R., *Seleção brasileira, 1914–2006*, Rio de Janeiro, Mauad, 2006

Pasolini, P.P., *Saggi sulla letteratura e sull'arte*, Milan, Meridiani Mondadori, 1999

Pereira, L.M., *Neymar Total*, Prime Books, 2013

Storti, V. & Fontanelle, A., *Campeonato Paulista*, São Paulo, Publifolha, 1997

Tejedor, J., *Neymar, Ousadia e Alegria*, Barcelona, Editorial Base, 2013

Tostão, *A Perfeição Não Existe – Paixão do Futebol por um Craque da Crônica*, São Paulo, Três estrelas, 2012

Wisnik, J.M., *Veneno Remédio: O Futebol e o Brasil*, São Paulo, Companhia das Letras, 2008

Newspapers
Brazil
O Globo
Estado do São Paulo
Jornal do Brasil
Folha de São Paulo
A Tribuna
O Diario
Lance

Spain
El País
El Mundo
Sport
Mundo Deportivo

Marca
AS

Italy
La Repubblica
Corriere della Sera
La Gazzetta dello Sport
Corriere dello Sport
Tuttosport

France
Le Monde
L'Equipe

USA
New York Times

Magazines
Placar (Brazil)
Veja (Brazil)
Select (Brazil)
Época (Brazil)
ISTOÉ (Brazil)
Gatopardo (Colombia)
France Football (France)
World Soccer (England)
Four Four Two (England)
Panenka (Spain)
Time (USA)

TV
Rete Globo (Brazil)
SportTV (Brazil)

ESPN (Brazil)
FOX Deportes (Argentina)
Barça TV (Spain)
Canal Plus (Spain)

Film
Santos 100 anos de futebol arte, directed by Lina Chamie,
produced by Canal Azul, co-produced by ESPN Brazil,
Grupo Bandeirantes de Comunicação

Web
www.fifa.com
www.cfb.com.br
www.conmebol.com
www.santosfc.com.br
www.fcbarcelona.cat
www.neymaroficial.com

Acknowledgements

I would like to thank Juca Kfouri, Martín Fernández, Paulo Coelho, Gian Oddi, Álex Sabino, José Miguel Wisnik, Newton Glória Lobato Filho, Pintado, Moacir Teixeira, Atilio Suarti, Maria Antonia Julião Faracco, Betinho, Fino, Edu Marangon, Manuel, Elton Luiz, Alcides Macrí, Lima, Lino Martins, Vágner Mancini, Dorival Júnior, Muricy Ramalho, Victor Andrade, Ricardo Rosa, Armênio Neto, Pepe, Zito, Tostão, Robinho, Léo Baptistão, Walter Casagrande, Luiz Felipe Scolari, Vicente del Bosque, Leda Catunda, Francisco Bosco, Allan Sieber, Hilário Franco Júnior, Cosme Salles, Didí, Alexandre Esnarriaga, Helena Passarelli, Alexandre Barreira, Thiago Campos, Darwin Valente, Manuel Giménez, Dolores de Haro, Duncan Heath, Robert Sharman, Charlie Wright, Laure Merle d'Aubigné and Roberto Domínguez.

Dedicated to Olmo, Lorenzo, Elvira, Alda and Tullio.